SaltandLight

SaltandLight

Living the
Sermon on the Mount

Eberhard Arnold

Foreword by Jürgen Moltmann

The Plough Publishing House

First edition 1967
Second edition, paperback 1977
Third edition, paperback 1986
Fourth edition, paperback 1998
Sixth printing, paperback 1999

Chapters five, six, and seven of the Gospel of Matthew have been reprinted from the *Revised Standard Version of the Bible*, © 1946, 1952, by Division of Christian Education of the National Council of Churches. Used with permission.

The verses quoted at the end of *The Fight Against Mammon* (James 5: 1–7) have been reprinted from *Holy Bible, New International Version®*, ©1973, 1978, 1984, by International Bible Society. Used by permission of International Bible Society.

All other Bible quotations were freely quoted in German by the author and translated by the editors.

Cover photograph: © IFA — Peter Arnold, Inc.

A catalog record for this book is available from the British Library.

Library of Congress Cataloging-in-Publication Data

Arnold, Eberhard, 1883–1935.
    [Salz und Licht. English]
    Salt and light: Living the Sermon on the Mount /
Eberhard Arnold; foreword by Jürgen Moltmann. — 4th ed.
        p. cm.
    ISBN 0-87486-099-7 (pbk.)
    1. Sermon on the mount.   I. Title.
BT380.A713   1997
226.9'06—dc21

                                                98-35117
                                                CIP

Printed in the USA

WE HAVE LISTENED to the Sermon on the Mount and perhaps have understood it. But who has heard it aright? Jesus gives the answer at the end (Matt. 7:24–29). He does not allow his hearers to go away and make of his sayings what they will, picking and choosing from them whatever they find helpful and testing them to see if they work. He does not give them free rein to misuse his word with their mercenary hands, but gives it to them on condition that it retains exclusive power over them.

Humanly speaking, we could understand and interpret the Sermon on the Mount in a thousand different ways. Jesus knows only one possibility: simple surrender and obedience, not interpreting it or applying it, but doing and obeying it. That is the only way to hear his word. He does not mean that it is to be discussed as an ideal; he really means us to get on with it.

Dietrich Bonhoeffer

To the Reader

Salt and Light became a book many years after Eberhard Arnold's death. Its chapters were compiled and translated by members of the Bruderhof communities from articles, talks, and lectures from the years 1915–1935. Arnold grappled with the Sermon on the Mount his whole adult life. His relentless faithfulness to its demands bore practical fruit in a community movement that is still thriving today. Although Arnold was addressing a Germany in political and social ferment, his words are not bound to time and place. They direct us out of our bankruptcy to a new, revolutionary way.

Contents

Foreword

THIS BOOK OPENS with the question, "How do we respond to the Sermon on the Mount?" – a question that must be asked by each new generation. Each generation must find its own answer to the call of Jesus. Yet throughout the centuries there is a fellowship of those who face the powerful challenge of the Sermon on the Mount without reservation, ready for unconditional discipleship. Among those who speak to us today are the Waldensians and Hussites, the Baptizers and the Hutterites, the Mennonites and Quakers, and now Eberhard Arnold of the Bruderhof. On the way of Jesus, however, intervals of time lose their meaning; brothers and sisters of earlier days speak to us as if they were present today – which they are, if we listen to them and through their voices hear the voice of Jesus.

As I was reading Arnold's vision of the Sermon on the Mount and imagining the first Bruderhof – a lonely, impoverished little settlement in the Rhön hills – I was suddenly struck by the inseparable connection between Jesus' words and unconditional discipleship, between discipleship and the communal life of the Twelve, between the life of brotherly love and the expectation of God's kingdom on earth. These things must never be separated.

Arnold shows us that the Sermon on the Mount is not a new moral law but a proclamation, a witness to the power of the coming kingdom and true life. The Beatitudes come before Jesus' new commandments. Before laying the yoke of discipleship upon us, Jesus fills our hearts with the powers of God's spirit. Arnold shows us that following these commandments consistently is neither an ideal nor an ordeal, but a matter of course in the community of Jesus. In the community of Jesus, life becomes clear, simple, decisive, and unequivocal. Gone are the many doubts and compromises, the many half-truths and the half-heartedness. We can only love God with our whole heart and strength; we can follow Jesus only with undivided dedication – otherwise we are not following him at all.

Arnold shows us further that discipleship and community life belong together: they cannot be separated. It is from community life that we draw the strength for discipleship and courage to face the inevitable opposition. In discipleship we find our brothers and sisters of the communal life. The Bruderhof community proves that. I ask myself what the state churches, still trying to lead a Christian life, can learn from such consistently Christian communities. First of all we have to lay down our old prejudices and heretic-hunting. The closely related Mennonite and Hutterite groups have never – neither in the past nor today – been fanatic enthusiasts or narrow

sectarians, but genuine Christian communities. True,
their existence represents a criticism of the life of Christians in the established churches. The answer will be to
begin learning from them. So I have been asking myself,
how can the established institutional church become a
living, communal church? How can our church parishes
become communities of faith and of life? I believe that
this is the way into the future, and I see more and more
people going in that direction. We are not looking for
the self-righteous Christian sect that despises the world,
but for the open church of the coming kingdom of God.
This church is open and welcomes everyone, like the
Bruderhof does. It is open to the poor, the handicapped,
and the rejected, who find a refuge and new hope there
because they find Jesus.

Arnold places much emphasis on the realism of Christian hope: Christians do not hope for salvation for their
souls in the hereafter, but pray, as Jesus bids us: "Thy
kingdom come!" Arnold has often called this coming
kingdom "God's future state." Like the New Testament,
he speaks of "the heavenly city" and "the heavenly
politeuma." He speaks of the kingdom that is to come to
earth in political terms. That is very important to me: if I
pray for the advent of this kingdom, I cannot abandon
the earth to wars and ecological destruction and to those
who hope for security by threatening such disasters. If I
pray for the coming of God's kingdom, I cannot stand by

while the environment and my fellow creatures are being annihilated through the progress of civilization and nuclear power stations. Praying for the coming of God's kingdom calls for a decisive resistance to the destruction of the earth. In his hope Arnold was as earthly, physical, and holistic as Christoph Blumhardt was.

Arnold once called the Bruderhof "a seed of God's kingdom." During the Nazi years this seed "died" like the buried grain of seed the apostles speak of. But it has also borne – and is bearing – rich fruits, not the least of which is hope. The Bruderhofs, like all faith-based communities and fellowships, are lights of hope in an age that sometimes looks very dark. May they no longer remain "hidden under a bushel," but be heeded more and more by the rest of us.

Jürgen Moltmann
Tübingen, Germany

Introduction

THOUGH LITTLE is known about him today, Eberhard
Arnold (1883–1935) was widely sought after during
his lifetime as a public speaker, lecturer, and publisher
in his native Germany. During and after his studies at
Breslau, Halle, and Erlangen (where he received his doc-
torate in 1909), he was active in the student revival
movement then sweeping those towns and became sec-
retary of the German Christian Student Union. In 1916
he became literary director of the Furche Publishing
House in Berlin, and editor of its monthly periodical.

Like thousands of young Germans in the 1920s, Eberhard and his wife Emmy were disillusioned by the failure
of the establishment – especially the churches – to provide answers to the problems of society in the turbulent
years following World War I. In their seeking, they were
influenced by the German Youth Movement (in which
Eberhard was a nationally-known participant), the German pastor Johann Christoph Blumhardt and his son
Christoph Friedrich, the sixteenth-century Anabaptists,
and, most significantly, the early Christians.

Eberhard has described this time of serious seeking in
this way:

> I would like to tell about my personal seeking. A group of
> young people often gathered around me, and I tried by

means of Bible studies and talks to lead people to Jesus. But after a while this was no longer enough. I found myself in a very difficult situation, and I was deeply unhappy. I began to recognize the needs of people in a deeper way: the need of their bodies and souls, their material and social need, their humiliation, exploitation, and enslavement. I recognized the tremendous power of mammon, discord, hate, and violence, and saw the hard boot of the oppressor upon the neck of the oppressed. If a person has not experienced these things, he might think such words an exaggeration – but these are the facts.

Then, from 1913 to 1917, I sought painfully for a deep understanding of the truth. I recognized more and more that personal dedication to people's souls was not all that Jesus asked – that it did not fully express the being of God. I felt that I was not fulfilling God's will by approaching people with a purely personal Christianity and concerning myself with individuals so that they, like myself, might come to this personal Christianity. During those four years I went through a hard struggle. I searched not only in the old writings, in Jesus' Sermon on the Mount and other scriptures, but I also wanted to get to know the life of the working classes – the oppressed humanity of the present social order – and to share in their life. I wanted to find a way that corresponded to the way of Jesus, of Francis of Assisi, and also the way of the prophets.

Shortly before the outbreak of the war [World War I], I wrote to a friend saying that I could not go on like this. I had interested myself in individuals, preached the gospel, and endeavored in this way to follow Jesus. But I had to find a way actually to serve humankind; I wanted a dedication that would establish a tangible reality by which men could recognize the cause for which Jesus died.

The war continued and we saw ever greater horrors. We saw the condition of the men who came back home. One young officer came home with both his legs shot off. Returning to his fiancée, he hoped to receive the loving care he so badly needed from her, but she informed him that she had become engaged to a man with a healthy body.

Then hunger came to Berlin. People ate turnips morning, noon, and night. When the people turned to the officials for money or food, they were told, "If you are hungry, eat turnips!" On the other hand, even in the middle of Berlin there were still well-to-do "Christian" families who had a cow and had milk when no one else did. Carts went through the streets bearing the bodies of children who had died. The bodies were wrapped in newspaper, for there was neither time nor money for a coffin. In 1917 I saw a horse collapse in the street: the driver was knocked aside by the starving people, who rushed to cut chunks from the warm body to bring home to their families.

During this time I visited a poor woman in a basement dwelling. Water was running down the walls of her cellar room. Although she was tubercular, her relatives were living in the same room with her. One could hardly have the window open because dirt would be kicked in by the people walking past in the street above. I offered to find her a different place to live, but you should have heard what she said: "I'm not going to make a fool of myself. I'll die here where I have lived." She was a living corpse.

After such experiences – and those of the revolutionary times, when working people were offered huge rooms and halls with parquet floors – I realized that the whole situation was unbearable. A leader of the Student Christian Movement told me that a high government official had agreed to work with me, provided I remain silent on the social issues: the war and the terrible suffering.

In the meetings we had at our home in Berlin, where we discussed all these things with our friends, it soon became clear that Jesus' way is a practical one: he has shown us a way of life that is more than a way of concern for the soul. It is a way that simply says, "If you have two coats, give one to him who has none; give food to the hungry, and do not turn away your neighbor when he needs to borrow from you. When you are asked for an hour's work, give two. You must strive for His justice. If you want to found a family, see that all others who want to found a family are able to do so, too. If you wish for education, work, and satisfying activity, make these possible for other people as well. If you say it is your duty to care for your health, then accept this duty for the health of others also. Treat people in the same way that you would be treated by them. This is the law and the prophets. Enter through this narrow gate, for it is the way that leads to the kingdom of God."

When this became clear to us, we realized that a person can go this way only when he or she becomes as poor as a beggar and takes upon himself, as Jesus did, the whole religious and moral need of mankind. Then we bear suffering, and we suffer because we see how injustice rules the world. Our hearts will be undivided only when we hunger for justice more than for water and bread. Then we will be persecuted for the sake of this justice. Only then will our righteousness be greater than that of the moralists and theologians. We will be filled with a new fire and a new spirit and warmth from the vital energy of God because we have received the Holy Spirit.

In this connection it became clear to us that the first Christian community in Jerusalem was more than a historical happening: it was here that the Sermon on the Mount came to life. We saw that it was more necessary than ever to renounce the last vestiges of privileges and rights and to let ourselves be won for this way of total love: the love that will pour itself out over the land from the breath of the Holy Spirit, the love that was born out of the first church community.

So we felt that we could not endure the life we were living any longer. We had to witness to the fact that Jesus concerned himself not only with people's souls but with their bodies as well. He made the blind see, the lame walk, and the deaf hear. And he prophesied a kingdom, a rule of God which was to change completely the conditions and the order of the world and make them new. To acknowledge this and live according to it – this, I believe, is God's command for the hour.

In 1920, out of a burning desire to practice the demands of the Sermon on the Mount, the Arnolds with their five children and a few other people began a communal life in the village of Sannerz. The community, which supported itself by agriculture and a small but vibrant publishing house, attracted thousands of visitors and grew quickly. By 1926 the house in Sannerz had become too small, and the next year a new Bruderhof (place of brothers) was started in the nearby Rhön hills.

The 1930s brought persecution by the National Socialist regime and expulsion from Germany. After a temporary stay in the neighboring country of Liechtenstein, the Bruderhof members fled to England, where they established a new community. Here the first major undertaking of the publishing house was the translation of several of Eberhard Arnold's most important works, including some of the articles and talks in this volume. World War II drove the Bruderhof to Paraguay in 1940, and in 1954 the first Bruderhof was established in the United States. Now, as we stand on the brink of a new millennium, we offer you this volume, affirming with Eberhard Arnold:

> We believe in this new birth – a life of light from God. We believe in a future of love and constructive fellowship. We believe in the peace of God's kingdom, and that he will come to this earth. This faith does not mean we are imagining things only for the future – God will bring this future and give us his heart and spirit today. Christ lives in his church, which is the hidden, living seed of the future kingdom. The peace that is characteristic of the church and the love-spirit of the future have been entrusted to her. Therefore she shows herself in the present as justice, peace, and joy in this world.

The Editors, 1998

The Sermon on the Mount

MATTHEW 5 – 7

SEEING THE CROWDS, he went up on the mountain, and when he sat down his disciples came to him. And he opened his mouth and taught them, saying:

Blessed are the poor in spirit, for theirs is the kingdom of heaven.

Blessed are those who mourn, for they shall be comforted.

Blessed are the meek, for they shall inherit the earth.

Blessed are those who hunger and thirst for righteousness, for they shall be satisfied.

Blessed are the merciful, for they shall obtain mercy.

Blessed are the pure in heart, for they shall see God.

Blessed are the peacemakers, for they shall be called sons of God.

Blessed are those who are persecuted for righteousness' sake, for theirs is the kingdom of heaven.

Blessed are you when men revile you and persecute you and utter all kinds of evil against you falsely on my account. Rejoice and be glad, for your reward is great in heaven, for so men persecuted the prophets who were before you.

You are the salt of the earth; but if the salt has lost its taste, how shall its saltness be restored? It is no longer good for anything except to be thrown out and trodden under foot by men.

You are the light of the world. A city set on a hill cannot be hid. Nor do men light a lamp and put it under a bushel, but on a stand, and it gives light to all in the house. Let your light so shine before men, that they may see your good works and give glory to your Father who is in heaven.

Think not that I have come to abolish the law and the prophets; I have come not to abolish them but to fulfil them. For truly, I say to you, till heaven and earth pass away, not an iota, not a dot, will pass from the law until all is accomplished. Whoever then relaxes one of the least of these commandments and teaches men so, shall be called least in the kingdom of heaven; but he who does them and teaches them shall be called great in the kingdom of heaven. For I tell you, unless your righteousness exceeds that of the scribes and Pharisees, you will never enter the kingdom of heaven.

You have heard that it was said to the men of old, "You shall not kill; and whoever kills shall be liable to judgment." But I say to you that every one who is angry with his brother shall be liable to judgment; whoever insults his brother shall be liable to the council, and whoever says, "You fool!" shall be liable to the hell of fire. So if you are offering your gift at the altar, and there remember that your brother has something against you, leave your gift there before the altar and go; first be reconciled to your brother, and then come and offer your gift. Make friends quickly with your accuser, while you are going with him to court, lest your accuser hand you over to the judge, and the judge to the guard, and you be put in prison; truly, I say to you, you will never get out till you have paid the last penny.

You have heard that it was said, "You shall not commit adultery." But I say to you that every one who looks at a woman lustfully has already committed adultery with her in his heart. If your right eye causes you to sin, pluck it out and throw it away; it is better that you lose one of your members than that your whole body be thrown into hell. And if your right hand causes you to sin, cut it off and throw it away; it is better that you lose one of your members than that your whole body go into hell.

It was also said, "Whoever divorces his wife, let him give her a certificate of divorce." But I say to you that every one who divorces his wife, except on the ground of unchastity, makes her an adulteress; and whoever marries a divorced woman commits adultery.

Again you have heard that it was said to the men of old, "You shall not swear falsely, but shall perform to the Lord what you have sworn." But I say to you, Do not swear at all, either by heaven, for it is the throne of God, or by the earth, for it is his footstool, or by Jerusalem, for it is the city of the great King. And do not swear by your head, for you cannot make one hair white or black. Let what you say be simply "Yes"or "No"; anything more than this comes from evil.

You have heard that it was said, "An eye for an eye and a tooth for a tooth." But I say to you, Do not resist one who is evil. But if any one strikes you on the right cheek, turn to him the other also; and if any one would sue you and take your coat, let him have your cloak as well; and if any one forces you to go one mile, go with him two miles. Give to him who begs from you, and do not refuse him who would borrow from you.

You have heard that it was said, "You shall love your neighbor and hate your enemy." But I say to you, Love your enemies and pray for those who persecute you, so that you may be sons of your Father who is in heaven; for he makes his sun rise on the evil and on the good, and sends rain on the just and on the unjust. For if you love those who love you, what reward have you? Do not even the tax collectors do the same? And if you salute only your brethren, what more are you doing than others? Do not even the Gentiles do the same? You, therefore, must be perfect, as your heavenly Father is perfect.

Beware of practicing your piety before men in order to be seen by them; for then you will have no reward from your Father who is in heaven.

Thus, when you give alms, sound no trumpet before you, as the hypocrites do in the synagogues and in the streets, that they may be praised by men. Truly, I say to you, they have their reward. But when you give alms, do not let your left hand know what your right hand is doing, so that your alms may be in secret; and your Father who sees in secret will reward you.

And when you pray, you must not be like the hypocrites; for they love to stand and pray in the synagogues and at the street corners, that they may be seen by men. Truly, I say to you, they have their reward. But when you pray, go into your room and shut the door and pray to your Father who is in secret; and your Father who sees in secret will reward you.

And in praying do not heap up empty phrases as the Gentiles do; for they think that they will be heard for their many words. Do not be like them, for your Father knows what you need before you ask him. Pray then like this:

Our Father who art in heaven,
Hallowed be thy name.
Thy kingdom come,
Thy will be done,
On earth as it is in heaven.
Give us this day our daily bread;
And forgive us our debts,
As we also have forgiven our debtors;
And lead us not into temptation,
But deliver us from evil.

For if you forgive men their trespasses, your heavenly Father also will forgive you; but if you do not forgive men their trespasses, neither will your Father forgive your trespasses.

And when you fast, do not look dismal, like the hypocrites, for they disfigure their faces that their fasting may be seen by men. Truly, I say to you, they have their reward. But when you fast, anoint your head and wash your face, that your fasting may not be seen by men but by your Father who is in secret; and your Father who sees in secret will reward you.

Do not lay up for yourselves treasures on earth, where moth and rust consume and where thieves break in and steal, but lay up for yourselves treasures in heaven, where neither moth nor rust consumes and where thieves do not break in and steal. For where your treasure is, there will your heart be also.

The eye is the lamp of the body. So, if your eye is sound, your whole body will be full of light; but if your eye is not sound, your whole body will be full of darkness. If then the light in you is darkness, how great is the darkness!

No one can serve two masters; for either he will hate the one and love the other, or he will be devoted to the one and despise the other. You cannot serve God and mammon.

Therefore I tell you, do not be anxious about your life, what you shall eat or what you shall drink, nor about your body, what you shall put on. Is not life more than food, and the body more than clothing? Look at the birds of the air: they neither sow nor reap nor gather into barns, and yet your heavenly Father feeds them. Are you not of more value than they? And which of you by being anxious can add one cubit to his span of life? And why are you anxious about clothing? Consider the lilies of the field, how they grow; they neither toil nor spin; yet I tell you, even Solomon in all his glory was not arrayed like one of these. But if God so clothes the grass of the field, which today is alive and tomorrow is thrown into the oven, will he not much more clothe you, O men of little faith? Therefore do not be anxious, saying, "What shall we eat?" or "What shall we drink?" or "What shall we wear?" For the Gentiles seek all these things; and your heavenly Father knows that you need them all. But seek first his kingdom and his righteousness, and all these things shall be yours as well.

Therefore do not be anxious about tomorrow, for tomorrow will be anxious for itself. Let the day's own trouble be sufficient for the day.

Judge not, that you be not judged. For with the judgment you pronounce you will be judged, and the measure you give will be the measure you get. Why do you see the speck that is in your brother's eye, but do not notice the log that is in your own eye? Or how can you say to your brother, "Let me take the speck out of your eye," when there is the log in your own eye? You hypocrite, first take the log out of your own eye, and then you will see clearly to take the speck out of your brother's eye.

Do not give dogs what is holy; and do not throw your pearls before swine, lest they trample them underfoot and turn to attack you.

Ask, and it will be given you; seek, and you will find; knock, and it will be opened to you. For every one who asks receives, and he who seeks finds, and to him who knocks it will be opened. Or what man of you, if his son asks him for a loaf, will give him a stone? Or if he asks for a fish, will give him a serpent? If you then, who are evil, know how to give good gifts to your children, how much more will your Father who is in heaven give good things to those who ask him? So whatever you wish that men would do to you, do so to them; for this is the law and the prophets.

Enter by the narrow gate; for the gate is wide and the way is easy, that leads to destruction, and those who enter by it are many. For the gate is narrow and the way is hard, that leads to life, and those who find it are few.

Beware of false prophets, who come to you in sheep's clothing but inwardly are ravenous wolves. You will know them by their fruits. Are grapes gathered from thorns, or figs from thistles? So, every sound tree bears good fruit, but the bad tree bears evil fruit. A sound tree cannot bear evil fruit, nor can a bad tree bear good fruit. Every tree that does not bear good fruit is cut down and thrown into the fire. Thus you will know them by their fruits.

Not every one who says to me, "Lord, Lord," shall enter the kingdom of heaven, but he who does the will of my Father who is in heaven. On that day many will say to me, "Lord, Lord, did we not prophesy in your name, and cast out demons in your name, and do many mighty works in your name?" And then will I declare to them, "I never knew you; depart from me, you evildoers."

Every one then who hears these words of mine and does them will be like a wise man who built his house upon the rock; and the rain fell, and the floods came, and the winds blew and beat upon that house, but it did not fall, because it had been founded on the rock. And every one who hears these words of mine and does not do them will be like a foolish man who built his house upon the sand; and the rain fell, and the floods came, and the winds blew and beat against that house, and it fell; and great was the fall of it.

And when Jesus finished these sayings, the crowds were astonished at his teaching, for he taught them as one who had authority, and not as their scribes.

Matthew 5, 6, 7 (RSV)

Not a New Law

HOW DO WE RESPOND to the Sermon on the Mount? The Sermon on the Mount is the first step on the way of discipleship, and it is of decisive importance to me that our church consider this deeply. If we fully grasp the Sermon on the Mount and believe it, then nothing can frighten us – neither our own self-recognition, nor financial threats, nor our personal weakness.

The dedication demanded in the Sermon on the Mount is not a new law or moral teaching. Instead it is forgiveness. Its vital element is the light and warmth of the Holy Spirit. Here is Christ: the essence of salt, and the strength of the tree that bears good fruit. The Sermon on the Mount shows us the character of a community, which shines like a light for the whole world.

The Sermon on the Mount is not a high-tension moralism, but we must grasp it as the revelation of God's real power in human life. If we take our surrender to God seriously and allow him to enter our lives as light, as the only energy which makes new life possible, then we will be able to live the new life.

If we see the Sermon on the Mount as five new commandments, as the Tolstoyans do, we will fall right into a trap. For in his book *My Religion,* Leo Tolstoy lists the commandments of Jesus from the Sermon on the Mount as five new laws: peacefulness with others, sexual purity and marital faithfulness, the refusal to swear oaths, nonresistance to evil, and love for one's enemies. But Jesus shows us that the clarity and demands of the old laws are not weakened by his coming into the world; instead they are infinitely sharpened. Moreover, these are only five examples – there could be five hundred or five thousand – revealing the powerful effect of God's work in Christ.

His righteousness, his justice, is better than anything scholars or theologians could offer. It is something absolutely different, and it does not depend on moral intentions and good ideas. The righteousness of the law can be fulfilled only through a new, organic way of living, through a life from God that flares up like light and sears and purifies like salt. It is like a flame that shines, like the sap that pulses through a tree. It is life!

■ Spoken on October 27, 1935, at the Rhön Bruderhof.

Becoming True Men and Women

IT HAS BEEN SAID that we should become truly human and dedicate ourselves to all people. This true humanity is seen most clearly in Jesus Christ and his Sermon on the Mount. For this we must have the love that exists among children, for with them love rules without any special purpose.

If we can feel what it means to become truly human and to find the right attitude of serving all who suffer; if we can become united about what Jesus said and how he lived, and agree that his nature was clearly revealed in the Sermon on the Mount; if we can recognize that the child-like spirit of love is all we need – then we will know the spirit that leads to such a life, and we will feel very close to one another.

When I read the Sermon on the Mount at the end of the war, decisive things, impossible to express in a few words, became clear to me. It would be much better to read the Sermon on the Mount itself. However, I would like to re-count what impressed and influenced me so decisively that I still think about it night and day.

The justice and goodness and social love that Jesus speaks of in the Sermon on the Mount are quite different from the moral teaching, piety, and dogmatism of theologians and moralists. This is why Jesus speaks of the tree, the salt, the light, and the city. He is speaking of God and his spirit.

Jesus says, "Beware of the Pharisees and theologians: beware of the false moralists when their deeds do not correspond to their words. By the fruit the tree is known." When Jesus speaks of the salt, he says to those who are of his spirit, "You are the salt of the earth!" What does Jesus mean by salt? Jesus is talking about the nature or essence of something. You may not want to hear about God; but think of the intrinsic nature, the essence, of the only thing that can save the world. It is an elixir, but certainly not an elixir of the devil. This is the salt of the earth, the element that can transform the earth's total corruption and ruin and bring about its rebirth.

What is this element? Jesus describes it in the first sentences of his Sermon on the Mount, after which he immediately talks about salt. His first words tell us what we will be like when we have the spirit of Jesus Christ, how we will be when we belong to God's kingdom and his future. These words must burn in our hearts and become alive, for the heart is what Jesus speaks about.

Blessed are those who have heart. Blessed are those who love, who build up unity everywhere. Blessed are those who stand with the poor; blessed are those who themselves are poor as beggars. Blessed are those who know themselves as beggars before the Spirit. Blessed are those who are so poor that they hunger and thirst. Blessed are those who feel this hunger and thirst for justice, for the justice of the heart, of love, for the establishment of peace in unity. For they are the people who carry the pain of the world on their hearts, who carry the suffering of the world in their innermost being. They do not think of themselves, for their whole heart is turned toward others.

Yet they are the people who are misunderstood and persecuted because they love justice and do not take part in injustice. This is why they are the salt of the earth. They do not take part in the injustice of mammon. They have no wealth, no savings account, nothing in the bank, nothing invested in houses or land; they have nowhere to go when need comes to them. Jesus tells us not to gather riches on this earth, but to gather the fortune found in love. Let your whole fortune be love, so that wherever you go hearts will open to you. You will be met with hatred because you bring justice, and you will be persecuted and hounded to death for not taking part in injustice. But you will be received with great love in huts which are open for you, and you will be taken in because you bring love.

This is your treasure and your wealth. It will free you of all care. You will be close to nature. You will live with the flowers and the birds, and you will not worry about your clothes or food. You will be one with the birds that find their food, and in harmony with the flowers that are clothed more beautifully than any vain men or women.

This is the new character of salt; this is light. Light makes everything bright and clear. The light meant here is not a cold light. It is the glowing light of hearth and lamp, the light that shines from a ring of torches or that streams from the windows of houses where community is alive. It is the light of truth that exists in love, and the love that rejoices in truth, justice, and purity. It is not the sultry, gloomy love of emotional passion; this brings injustice. It is the love that lightens up faith, that brings clarity to everything. Light is like salt because salt consumes itself, just as a candle burns itself down.

In the Sermon on the Mount, which is a proclamation of love, Jesus speaks of adultery, which can also consist of thoughts and feelings of the heart. Adultery breaks a relationship of faithfulness, truthfulness, and responsible love. But light and salt overcome such things. The same is true when people swear oaths and make vows in order to be believed. Jesus says, "Just by this you prove that no one can believe you. Say simply yes or no. Be completely true."

People think they should love their friends, who show love to them. But Jesus says, "Love your enemies." This means that you can never kill anyone. You can never hurt or kill souls, for you must live in absolute love. This love will become so complete that you cannot go to law against another. If someone wants to take your cloak, take off your jacket and give that as well. If someone demands of you one hour's work, give two. It must be like this with everything. Your life will have a kind of perfection, although you will not be a saint. The perfection will consist in this: you will be very weak and you will make many mistakes; you will be awkward, for you will be poor in spirit and hunger and thirst for justice. You will not be perfect, but you will love. This is the gate and the way. Whatever you desire for yourself, wish the same for others. If you expect something from people, give the same to them.

There is nothing greater than love. There is nothing more holy than love. There is nothing more true than love, nothing more real. So let us hand our lives over to love and seal the bond of love.

■ Spoken at the Rhön Bruderhof, September 22, 1935, in response to visitors' questions.

Salt and Light

THE NATURE OF SALT is salt, or it is nothing. The essence of salt is its action. By itself it has no purpose. Salt is there for the sake of the whole.

Whoever receives God's life and grasps the nature of his future has taken on the character of salt. What is important to God is genuineness. He does not expect a person to adopt an attitude that is not in accord with his inner self and feelings. Christ sees in his friends those who have his spirit, who breathe his life. The powers of the future world are at work in them, revealing unconditional love, righteousness, and purity. The coming kingdom, which will encompass the whole earth, belongs to God. It opposes all decay; it resists death and all that is insipid, flabby, and weak.

Salt can delay death. We know that doctors postpone death and revive or maintain the regenerative power of an organ by injecting salt. The injustice of the world – sin itself – is the disease of the world's soul that leads to death. Our mission on behalf of the kingdom is to be the salt of the earth: to stem its injustice, prevent its decay, and hinder its death.

The world must perish in order to be born again. But as long as salt remains salt, it restrains the fulfillment of evil in the world and acts as the power that will one day renew the earth. If the church were no longer to act as salt, it would no longer be the church – it would succumb to death and have to be stamped out. If salt becomes taste-less, how shall it be salted? It is fit for nothing but to be trodden underfoot. Salt by its nature is entirely different from the food it makes palatable. So the salt of the earth should not expect the present age to turn into salt. But the presence of Jesus in the kingdom is a constant warning to the world that without salt it will die. As food is unpalat-able without salt, so is the world without the church. And while humankind cannot attempt to act as its own salt, it can recognize the character of death and decay and how it must be combated. A corrective is placed before humanity as a goal to live up to.

Salt can have power only as long as it is different from the surrounding mass and does not fall into decay itself. If it becomes tasteless, it must be spat out. The salt of the earth is where God is, where the justice of the future king-dom is lived out and the powers of the coming order pro-mote organic life and growth. In other words, salt is present where the victorious energy of God's love is at work. God himself is the creative spirit who overcomes corruption, the living spirit who wakens the dead. He is the God of miracles who can bring forth new birth out of corruption and degeneration, replacing nausea and disgust with joy and well being.

God's power, welling up from the depths to flood all of life, surpasses everything that rotten morality and hypocritical social conventions can achieve. God's word has the strength of salt: the manliness and austere courage that do not swim with the stream and are not infected with corruption. There is simple and concise speech and an unvarnished truthfulness (which, if it lacks love however, is deadly to both the speaker and the one spoken to). There is love that cannot harm, let alone kill, another human being, love that resolves rather to pluck out the evil eye than have it corrupt the whole body. There is loyalty and integrity that never changes, whose word and love stand forever. Finally, there is freedom from everything outward and unessential, a freedom that is ready to sacrifice all possessions and any amount of time, for it is love, love to enemies as well as to friends and brothers and sisters. It is freedom from earthly treasure, freedom from the cares and worries of possessions, a childlike joy in light and color, in God himself and all that he is and gives.

Only this God-given life is the salt that counteracts the spirit of the world, the salt that is death's mortal enemy. But salt can be nothing else but salt. Whoever has the spirit of Jesus acts spontaneously as salt. Anyone who wants to become salt without being salt from the source, from God, is a fool. When Christ said, "You are the salt of the earth…you are the light of the world," he was not demanding the impossible but expressing his deepest insight into the very nature of things.

THIS SALT, THIS LIFE, is the light that can be kindled only in fire. Without fire one cannot expect light. The dark planet Neptune cannot turn into a brilliant sun; neither can the cold light of the moon change into midday heat. Black coal can be ignited and turned into warmth-giving fire, but in order to give off the heat and light it must be burned and reduced to ashes.

A light on a candlestick consumes itself to give light to all in the house. It serves the intimate unity of the household because its life consists in dying. To spare the candle must necessarily mean to go without light. It would be sinful to cover up a burning light. Rob a burning candle of the air it needs to give light, and it goes out.

Light is characteristic of the people of Jesus in its total brightness and warmth. The old life, consumed, turns into life-giving strength. Shameful things can live only in the dark. Brightness leads to clarity and frankness, simplicity and purity, genuineness and truth. Where Jesus' influence makes people real, their life becomes genuine and pure. It shines into the darkness of the world around, unmasking everything that is spurious and untrue, everything that tries to hide.

The light Jesus kindles is never exhausted in making a situation clear. Cold light has no part in the kingdom of God. Intelligent recognitions, systematic clarity of thought, and sharp discernment – this is not what Jesus is talking about. We cannot try to think as God might through our power of reason. What matters is to live in and from God's heart. Like the sun, quickening warmth belongs to the brightness of his being. The light he gives creates community and draws people together in joy, with love flowing from the depths of their souls and finding expression in constructive deeds – deeds that build up and never destroy.

Sunlight sparkles with life and generates life on the earth, making it germinate and bear fruit everywhere. Those who live in the light belong to life and find their way in the sunlight. Night is dead because it is cold and dark. Yet even in the life of the light and sun there is a dying. Because our life moves between day and night, we can gain the life of resurrection only by dying.

No light can radiate brightness and warmth without consuming itself. The greatest Man, in giving light, suffered this most violently. The light of the world went forth from the cross of Jesus. Those who experience the world's suffering and guilt with the crucified Christ – and their own sin and forgiveness – are able to serve the world with the light and strength of the risen Lord. For after Christ rose from the grave, he sent his disciples to bear his light to the ends of the earth.

Christ himself is this light. It is the fire of judgment that comes over us to consume the old, rotten life, to lead us who are crucified with him into a radiant life of resurrection. For there is only one who is the light of the world and who shines on all who come into this world. He himself was all light. He was not entangled in untruthfulness or impurity, lovelessness or greed. It is an illusion to push the false light of our own life into the foreground, trying to shine without being consumed in Christ. No human being can teach us what light is. To give oneself, as the sun gives of itself to the earth, can never be our own doing.

Even the sun directs our gaze away from itself and to the life illumined by it. We speak of "sun" when we see the hills, woods, and fields glowing in the light. A city on the hill shines out for all to see; but no one would notice it unless the sun shone on it. Where the sun casts light and warmth, life is awakened and becomes an organic union of individual living beings. Where there is life there is fellowship.

Just as a light on a candlestick gathers the household, so the city on the hill is the shining image of community – an organic unity in its economy and management, community of work, and faith and joy. The towers of a city on the hill can be seen far and wide – signs of civic freedom, tokens of the city communality, and symbols of fellowship in faith. Such a city is not built to be hidden, to have an isolated life for itself. Its open gates show the joy of hearts open to everyone.

There is nothing hidden about Jesus – he wants nothing furtive. His light is an all-inclusive life force that affects all relationships in life, in the same way that the sun shines upon the just and the unjust. God does good to enemy and friend alike; he is there for everyone and everything. The task of his salt and his light, the task of the city on the hill, is to serve all.

Not a single area of life should remain unaffected by this salt and this light. There is no responsibility in public life, including economics and politics, from which the city on the hill may remain aloof. Nowhere should the poison of decay be allowed to set in without being counteracted by salt. No wickedness must be allowed to lurk in the dark. The light must scare away the horrors of night. The icy, deadly breath of hate or coldness of heart cannot take full possession of this earth so long as the warm love of Christ's light is not taken from it.

The secret of salt and radiating light lies in their unadulterated truthfulness and clarity. God's city on the hill has a concern and responsibility for all aspects of life, and for people in the most distant places. This responsibility, however, is quite different from that borne by the people themselves. The city on the hill has a freedom, an essential quality of fellowship, which it cannot forfeit to any kingdom of this world, any government, any church, any political party, or any other organization of this age. It serves the whole of life without letting itself be enslaved. It fights against all suffering and injustice without succumbing to the suffering and becoming unjust itself. It has to remain salt and light, for the seed of the future age lies hidden in it.

■ Published as "Licht und Salz" in the periodical *Das neue Werk,* 1920.

Happiness

JESUS SHOWED his friends and all who listened to him the nature of the coming world order and its people. At that time – as today – people were waiting for the new order to come to each heart, as well as into the political and economic structures of nations. People longed for the new kingdom of justice which the prophets had spoken of. They were convinced that the new justice had to be a social justice, set up on the laws of love and grace. In God's heart, justice and grace dwell so close to each other that both move the heart as though they were one.

Then Jesus came, and he disclosed the nature and practical consequences of this justice. He showed people that the justice of the future state must be completely different from the moralistic justice of the pious and holy, who felt that only they represented justice. He made it clear through his own nature and his words that God's justice is a living, growing power which develops organically within us, a process that conforms to sacred laws of life.

Therefore Jesus could not simply give the people commands about moral conduct. He came to them quite differently. He discerned the nature of those who possessed his righteousness. He told them how they would appear to others: blessed, happy are those who have this nature, for they see God; to them belongs the kingdom of the future; they shall inherit the earth; they shall be comforted and satisfied; as those born of God, they shall obtain mercy.

Jesus himself radiated the unity of all the characteristics of this spirit of the future. It is impossible to take any one sentence out of its context and set it up as a law on its own. If anyone places nonviolence or purity of heart or any other moral or political demand by itself and uses this to set up something new, he is on the wrong track. Certainly it is not possible to take part in God's kingdom without purity of heart, without vigorous work for peace; but unless the good tree is planted, the good fruit cannot be harvested. The change extends to all areas. It is a lost cause to try to follow Christ in only one sphere of life.

The Beatitudes cannot be taken apart. They portray the heart of the people of the kingdom – a heart whose veins cannot be dissected and pulled to pieces. Because of this the Beatitudes begin and end with the same promise of possessing the kingdom of heaven. Those who are blessed are characterized by their poverty and neediness, longing, hunger, and thirst. At the same time they possess wealth in love, energy for peace, and victory over all resistance. Their nature is purity and single-heartedness, in which they see God. These are people of inner vision, who see the essential. They bear the world's suffering. They know that they are beggars in the face of the Spirit. Knowing they have no righteousness within themselves, they look to righteousness, and they hunger and thirst for the Spirit. Theirs is not the happiness of satiety; it is not the pleasure of gratified desire. A deeper happiness is disclosed here to eyes and hearts that are open. Only where people feel poor, empty, hungry, and thirsty will there be an openness to God and his riches.

This is the essence of true religious experience: richness in God and poverty in oneself. These contrasting elements always belong together: becoming one with God, and yet always longing for him; firmness of heart, and weakness of soul; the justice of God's love, and the suffering of injustice. Wherever there is religious satiety and moral self-satisfaction, wherever political achievements or other good works create self-righteousness, wherever anyone feels rich or victorious, the happiness in the fellowship of the kingdom has been lost. Those who believe in the justice of God's future and know the happiness of his kingdom are guided by Jesus on the simple way of discipleship. They feel the injury of injustice in themselves and all around them, yet their hearts are fixed on the Spirit and his prophetic justice of love. They know the poverty of spirit in themselves and in all mankind, but they have a vision of the justice of God's kingdom and are comforted by the certainty that love shall conquer the earth.

So they are both poor and rich at the same time. They are people of faith who have nothing in themselves and yet possess everything in God. In spite of failing again and again, they try to reveal God's invisible nature through their deeds. Just as they themselves receive mercy, so they pour mercy on all in need. They are on the side of poverty and suffering, on the side of all who suffer injury, and they are ready to be persecuted with them for the sake of justice. They know that they cannot go through life without struggle and that their opponents' slander will fall on them like a hailstorm; yet they rejoice in this struggle and remain the peacemakers who overcome opposition everywhere and conquer enmity through love. The people of the Beatitudes are the people of love. They live from God's heart, and there they feel at home. The law of the spirit of life has set them free from the inescapable law of sin and death; no power can separate them from the love of God in Christ Jesus.

What is most remarkable and mysterious about these people is that they perceive everywhere the same seed of God. Where human beings break down under the suffering in the world, where hearts feel their own poverty and long for the Spirit, there they hear his footsteps in history; where the revolutionary desire for social justice arises, where a protest against war and bloodshed rings out, where people are persecuted because of their socialism or pacifism, and where purity of heart and compassion can be found – there they see the approach of God's kingdom and anticipate the bliss to come.

There is no other way to prepare inwardly for the coming kingdom than the way Jesus shows us here. Only by admitting our poverty of spirit can we start on this way. Everything else disappears and becomes nothing when we hunger and thirst for the justice of love. This is essential for opening our hearts to what God alone can give.

■ Published as "Das Glück" in *Das neue Werk,* 1920 / 21.

The Nature of
the New Justice

THE SERMON ON THE MOUNT reveals Jesus' heart and it confronts us with his will. The stage is set: the large crowd gathers and as Jesus speaks to the people, the disciples throng around him. Turning, he looks at each one as he speaks. This is the prelude to the great challenge of the Sermon on the Mount.

Jesus addresses everyone, but in the crowd he sees those who are or will become his disciples. He knows that all are poor and empty, but he brings happiness and wealth to those who – because they feel their poverty – are open to what he gives. The Sermon on the Mount is not a law, nor does it require a moral effort or an exertion of energy. It only requires emptiness, a vacuum – utter poverty which can achieve nothing and has nothing to show for itself.

In Luke this is written without qualification: Happy are you, the poor! Blessed are you who hunger and thirst! Blessed are you who weep! Blessed are you when you are persecuted! There is no hint of a specialized religious life. The mark of the citizens of the kingdom is the simple fact that they are poor, despised, and maligned; that they hunger and thirst and know suffering.

Luke cannot ignore the words: Woe to you that are rich! Woe to you that are full! Woe to you that laugh! Woe to you of whom people only speak well! This "Woe!" applies wherever anything is seen as a possession, as a substance of life, as admirable, even as a commonly recognized necessity. There the basic prerequisite for the kingdom – being empty – is lacking.

This poverty is disclosed in its depths as poverty of spirit, emptiness of conventional religion, morals, and wisdom. It is a mourning for the world, for collective and individual guilt, for material need, and for the deepest need of the soul. The persecution and contempt that follow must be persecution for the sake of that new justice, free of moralism. This justice will be hated most of all by those who want to be righteous in their wealth, morally correct, and religious.

The nature of this new justice is the theme of the Sermon on the Mount. It is blissfulness in poverty. It is the mystery of a changed heart, that radical change proclaimed by John the Baptist, the last prophet of the first Judaism. He foretold the new order of things, envisioned by all the prophets before him. He proclaimed that it would come down from heaven as the approach of God. He proclaimed God as joy for the individual, and justice and fellowship for all people. By his baptism, Jesus let

himself be immersed in this justice of the future, which is
God himself. This justice condemns to death the present
life on earth.

THE ENTIRE SERMON ON THE MOUNT shows us the characteristics of this new justice – a gift of the future, a promise
of God. The God of this goodness is the God of creation,
the ultimate mystery of life, the origin of procreation and
living growth. Thus this justice cannot exist where it is a
matter of the goodness and achievement of people as they
are. On earth this justice appeared only once, in the Son of
Man, in Jesus. It is present today in the risen Lord, active
in his spirit, working as the power of the creator, the God
of resurrection.

The Sermon shows us, then, the character of Jesus himself and therefore the character of his kingdom. Here
there can be no self-conscious awareness of human goodness or nobility, no standing on rights, and no opposition
between people. Here God's love gives strength and joy,
for here, having nothing means having everything.

An understanding of the Sermon on the Mount can be
given only to those who have reverence for the Creator:
who sense that all natural powers of body and soul are
also a gift from God and utterly dependent on him. God's
creation can never be brought about by human efforts.

The new creation in Christ's spirit has nothing to do with the efforts of people as they are today. Jesus does not say, "You should be light, you should be salt, you should make yourselves into a city!" He recognizes that the new creation is a being that stems from the Creator. "You are the salt of the earth; you are the light of the world." Light, like salt, does its task by consuming itself. The person who gives up his own life becomes happy doing so. The selfless devotion to the task of love is the essence of Jesus and his kingdom. Only out of such love can there be fellowship.

This new life of love that comes to men from God carries on its activity freely in unity and in work. To make a communal life like this is just as impossible as trying to produce a tree in a factory. Building up church community out of the spirit is the work of God, independent of human activity. Creation's law of growth and life is contrasted with human efforts, just as in the letter to the Romans the law of the spirit of life is contrasted with the law of sin and death.

What we cannot accomplish, God can accomplish. His creative spirit is the secret of the law of life, for God is a God of all that is living, not a God of death. The resurrection of Jesus is the ultimate revelation of this law of life.

The Sermon on the Mount can be grasped only where Jesus is proven powerfully to be the Son of God. Outside of this, the Sermon on the Mount remains an impossibility, a utopia or fantasy, self-deception or madness.

As a seed, buried in the soil, dies and then bursts forth bearing fruit for all, so also the life that springs from the Spirit is a gift that seeks to embrace all living things. It is the mortal enemy of death and does away with all hatred, murder, and human effort. This liberating love alone can be the fulfillment of life. Only the love of God that lifts us out of the human sphere affirms life and bestows its gifts on all that is living. Only God has this perfect life that sends his sun on all – on sinners and moralists, on the just and the unjust, on those who seek God and those who blaspheme him. This is what makes his justice so different from the moralists and theologians, who find it necessary to emphasize boundaries and differences.

God's heart is mercy. His love goes out to all. He wants justice in external things just as he wants mercy on the soul, because he is the "soul of mercy." Luke summarizes the attitude of the citizens of the kingdom with the simple words: Love! Be merciful from your hearts! Hold on to nothing for yourselves. Do not judge or seek faults in others. Give to all and be generous to your enemies.

This reconciliation and nonresistance means giving up all rights. It demands expending more time, more strength, and more life, even when the first step of giving oneself has provoked nothing but enmity. Opposition stimulates love to more energetic effort. The urge for dedication is only strengthened whenever it meets hostility.

There can be a living relationship only with neighbors and enemies. Jesus' witness turns to both with equal power. For Jesus, love to one's neighbor – which he equates with love to God – is inseparably bound to unconditional love to one's enemy. This love from God overflows on both sides. It is the love proclaimed in the Sermon on the Mount to both neighbors and enemies and proves itself as faithfulness and truthfulness. The marriage vow and the simple yes and no of daily life symbolize the faithfulness of love through the joys and the struggles of human relationships.

Those of us who dare to live by this spirit stand again and again before the infinite, the boundless. We tremble as before a bottomless abyss, for on this way there are no footholds. And yet our lungs fill up over and over again with endless purity and strength, for the air which this spirit wafts to us is the eternal breath of God; it is God himself as spirit. But again, it threatens to burst us apart, for our lungs cannot contain the infinite. On this way we are simultaneously condemned and pardoned, poverty-stricken and excessively rich, put to death and awakened.

The laws of antipathy and elective affinity yield, for no one is seen as more valuable than another. Neither do economic problems stop us.

That which is loud and conspicuous must end, for creation takes place in quiet – germinating life is hidden. Humans cannot hear the harmony of the cherubim and galaxies in their eternal worship of God. So too, in the life that comes from God, prayer is chaste and hidden. The Father looks for life in what is hidden. The remote mountain, the barren steppe, and the closed room are the places of final decision. These secluded hours are brief and clear. Their content is simple and concerned with one thing alone: the kingdom of God on earth, and that his will is done on earth. This will bring about the transformation of all relationships, daily bread for all, and forgiveness and protection for his people.

THE SERMON ON THE MOUNT LIES at the heart of the proclamation of John the Baptist: change yourselves fundamentally, for the kingdom of God is near. This means that we must seek protection from the hour of temptation, for it will come, bringing a catastrophic revolution over the whole earth. Out of the urgency of this final decision, a new attitude of trust must be born: voluntary poverty as the expression of trust and devotion.

Gather no riches for yourselves! Know only the one treasure, the treasure in heaven. Your longing can have only one object. Your heart is either set on things, or else it is directed toward something entirely different. A divided heart leads to darkness and judgment. You can never serve

God and money at the same time. What the heart longs for is decisive. Consequently, your worry about material things and your existence stems from the same godless spirit of mammon as accumulating wealth. Life that is given by God liberates from both worry and possession. Just as the birds and flowers in creation are cared for, so in the new creation there is abundance of food and clothing for those who trust in God and acknowledge his kingdom as the first and last.

On this way a simple rule of life arises naturally: never burden yourselves by looking far ahead; always live one day at a time. If you can do this, you will live like children, birds, and flowers – for them each day is a lifetime. Every day unfolds new joy and new hope even if every day may have brought you new shadows and new nightfall. Every day you may have broken down in guilt and failure. In the face of the Sermon on the Mount, every day may have shown you your helplessness a thousandfold. Yet each new day brings new sun, new air, and new grace.

So trust grows, trust in God and in those in whom God is at work. Jesus encourages those who obey him to pray and believe again and again. He promises that when we ask, it shall be given. To those who knock it will be opened, and they will enter, like going through an open gate into a large garden – God's garden. The gate is narrow, but it is there for all.

Luke says clearly what the object of this asking, believing, waiting, and daring is. It is the Spirit! If you who are evil give your children good things, truly you can rely on God to give you what you need – the Holy Spirit. Everything contained in the Sermon on the Mount is done by this Spirit, which has the nature of a lamb. In the Spirit, the material form of God's new creation arises; it transforms wolves into lambs, and man's predatory world into God's kingdom of peace.

Nobody should be deceived, however, by signs and gestures, busyness and bustle. Jesus warns against being deceived by soft, lamb-like words, while the unbroken wolf nature lies in ambush. Its character is the grasping, rapacious will. But we must distinguish the spirits and not give what is holy to dogs; at the same time, we cannot judge. For a judge does not stand with the condemned: he speaks out a final verdict, and trust is destroyed. No one has the right to do this. We human beings are all alike, we all sit on the same bench. Only God judges in such a way that he redeems.

The Sermon on the Mount judges us all, for it shows us our evil fruits by which the evil tree is recognized. The good fruit of the deed and the new love for all that flows from the heart is what marks the new life spoken of in the Sermon on the Mount. Where these words of Jesus become life and action, there is God's firm building, which cannot be overthrown even in the final catastrophe. Where his words do not become action, the only thing that can be expected is a heap of rubble – which is what human deeds truly are.

■ Published as "Die Bergrede, ein Zeugnis vom Osterkursus in Sannerz, 1922" in *Das neue Werk,* 1922.

"But I Say to You..."

CHAPTER SIX

U NTIL JESUS APPEARED, the greatest goodness anyone could offer God was moral endeavor, ethical striving, strenuous efforts toward an ideal goal, and scrupulous obeying of commands and prohibitions. People strove to express or stifle contrary inclinations, or frantically attempted to deny and mortify the flesh. They labored in human strength to scale a mountain where the light would not be obscured nor the air polluted.

Jesus brings a justice better than anything human effort can achieve, and different in every sense from what the law and the prophets offer. Even so, the law and the prophets reveal God's being and will. Jesus does not undo or obscure in any way the incorruptible clarity of this revelation. Those who try to oppose God's clear will by confusing or breaking down these moral commandments are desecrating that which God has laid in their conscience. Devoid of this sanctuary in the conscience, they lose their security against the sinister powers of lying, hate, and greed, which then hound them from one situation to another until finally, without support, they fall prey to death.

It remains that not one letter of these ethical commands and moral prohibitions will be canceled until the essential spirit of these laws has been revealed and has taken on flesh and life. These commands express the holy "thou shalt" of our inner calling, the holy "must" of our inner destiny, the only absolute that lives in the human soul. Today more and more people reject one after the other of these laws and declare them null and void. They will be poorly prepared for God's kingdom.

Until God's word became flesh and reality in Jesus, God chose to express the essence of his holiness in an almost petrified form, demanding and forbidding. No being existed that could embody God's holiness and perfect clarity. God's will had to be expressed in the letter of the law tablets, because there was no living heart to give it expression in a genuine way.

Where greed still rules and the truthfulness and purity of Jesus has not yet taken root, the law must take over if all is not to be destroyed. The state with its violence and the law with its statute books are a necessary safety valve for the chaotic, inorganic mass of people. Just as steam can burst a boiler and evaporate, so the opposing elements in society could burst and ruin everything without the iron boiler of governmental force and the safety valves of its laws.

All of life is different as soon as people are gripped by God's love. They grow close to one another and become organs of a mystical body, ruled by a spirit of unity – one heart and one soul. The necessity for force and coercion, for law and moral striving, is removed because the true spirit, which the law expressed imperfectly, comes to rule. Jesus brought the new righteousness – goodness of heart and organic strength from God – which embraces all human existence. It is the justice of the future and no longer needs to take into account the restraints and injuries that are part of our present legal relationships.

This new justice is unconquerable because it is God's goodness. It can be neither weakened nor changed, for it manifests a life energy that wants to unfold in every area of life. This justice is goodness, because God is good. His goodness is love. His justice reveals all the powers of love. Any attempt to reach this goodness on the basis of legal rules or regulations is doomed to failure, for that kind of justice could never be bursting, overflowing life. It could produce nothing but laborious pressure to fit into patterns that do not spring from life itself.

The scribes and Pharisees had a firm conviction, a moral direction, and an iron will. They were better than their reputation; they were morally upright, devout figures who commanded respect, men who felt deeply their responsibility for their people. But what they lacked was the free spirit blowing from God, the gift of life, the life that grows and bears fruit just because it is there. They lacked being filled with the Holy Spirit, God himself.

God's nature cannot be imitated or created, and nothing can replace his power. So too, the works of the first love cannot be artificially manufactured. No intelligent reflection, no resolution or effort, can produce the warmth of heart that is of God and which replaces morals and the law. Jesus overcomes morals and moralism by something better – God's own life. Where he is alive, active love takes the place of dead moralism.

Jesus brings a totally different righteousness because he brings God himself, who encompasses everything and tolerates nothing isolated. He brings the God of radiating light and flooding warmth; the living God, who wants nothing but life; the God of riches, whose being consists in giving. Those who lose themselves in God have the new justice. Where God himself lives and works, this justice of the warmly pulsing heart replaces the stony tablets of the law.

■ Published as "Die bessere Gerechtigkeit" in *Das neue Werk,* 1920.

Away from
Compromise and Shadow

WE MUST WRESTLE with the question of compromise because it comes up everywhere and concerns serious-minded people again and again. Behind it the fundamental problem of life lies dormant: the question of evil and death. Evil and death are so oppressive that goodness and life are constantly threatened with falling victim to them. But it is frightening to see an increasing apathy and compromise with darkness – an avoidance of the either-or of life and death.

There can be no compromise with evil! The word compromise has its origin in the language of law: a mutual settlement between contending parties. It belongs, as the only settlement between opposing parties, where there is legal conflict. A court of arbitration must insist on compromise.

The question is whether one can replace this highest legal justice with a better justice – the justice of Jesus' heart, as revealed in the Sermon on the Mount. This means that when faced with the threat of a legal battle, the one who wants the way of life and love must give up everything rather than compromise, and must allow the opponent to take everything away. If we do this we will be met, not by hard demands on our futile efforts, but by opportunities for overflowing love and joy.

This is news of the new life: bringing joy excludes murder; love hates no man; truth strikes no compromise with lying; the heart remains pure only by making no concessions; the Father of Jesus who gives everything makes no settlement with mammon. Joy in life and love for all tolerates no compromise with evil, no concession to loveless indifference or murderous injustice, because love touches all things and changes all relationships. This is the message of the kingdom, the character of Jesus' words. Here is his heart.

Every movement that stems from God points to this way. Whenever a living movement of heart dies, Christ's way is forsaken. The process of dying reaches its final stage when there is no more wrestling with death, when the struggle for life is deserted and people surrender unresisting to the shadow of death. This includes the inevitable dying that threatens every movement as soon as materialism and mediocrity gain a foothold and we avoid the struggle to which Jesus has called us.

TODAY PEOPLE TRY to live simultaneously on the basis of law and of grace. A life of nonviolence is called absurd even though Jesus lived such a life. People oppose an uncompromising stand, calling it legalism and fanaticism.

They say an unqualified yes to materialism, are infatuated with sin, and take pains to show that one can never get rid of it. It basically makes no difference to them whether there is more compromise or less, which all shows how far they are from the way.

Only love as experienced in the full forgiveness of sin can bring healing. In this atmosphere the legalistic "thou shalt" and "thou shalt not" cease to exist. This cannot be emphasized strongly enough. Yet it is not convincing if the experience of this love does not lead to consequences in practical life. He who is forgiven much loves much. How can we love God, whom we do not see, if we do not love the brother or sister whom we do see?

There is only one way – the way of love – that comes from forgiveness and has its essence in forgiveness. This way is absolute discipleship of Jesus. It makes no compromises with our cold and loveless age. This does not mean that the person gripped by love never makes compromises; rather, the love that has gripped him or her can make no compromises. If evil deeds are done, they come from depravity and weakness of character. But when love takes hold again, the highest goal reappears and the heart lives again – full and glowing. The words of Jesus bring back the power of perfect love.

The first letter of John describes this uncompromising attitude: whoever claims to be without sin is a liar. We are told this so that we may not sin. But if we do sin, we have an advocate who expiates the sin of the whole world. Whoever abides in him does not sin. If any one sins, then in this sin he has not seen and known him. "We know that we are of God, and the whole world is in the power of evil."

Those who defend sin show that they have gone astray and lost sight of Jesus. They neither see nor recognize him. There is a great deal of difference between doing evil, or turning our backs on it and forgetting it. For Paul it was essential to leave everything behind and to race single-minded toward the goal. Certainly it was always clear to him – and he testified to it strongly – that this did not mean he had no guilt. But the forgiveness that Christ brings means liberation from wrong and evil. Paul was a fighter in full armor who fought against all evil and even against death itself.

IT IS SIGNIFICANT that uncompromising love has nothing to do with softness or indecision in the face of battle. On the contrary, those who are resolute have to carry on a spiritual fight against all spiritual powers that oppose peace and love. In this fight it is out of the question to injure or kill one's fellow men. No human judgment can declare them as evil, rejected, or condemned to death. Therefore, this spiritual fight must be waged all the more sharply in each person and against everything that is injurious to life, hostile to fellowship, and against God.

Whoever is full of life and gripped by love is a fighter to the point of death. He is never hard toward others, though it may be felt as hardness when he struggles with passionate love against the evil in himself, in others, and in public affairs. This fight is not only a private matter between him and God; it must also be a public striving against the evil in all human and social conditions.

Those who fight for love in this way will be wrongly seen as moralistic or even legalistic. Their conduct toward people and all human works and institutions is defined by the goal of God's kingdom. Their ethics will be determined by the character of the Son of Man and his followers, by the truth of love, and by the will of God's heart. They must live a life of love in the attitude of the future world and in the perfection of God, because there is no other life.

This brings us to an age-old topic: perfection. Certainly as we are there is no state of sinlessness. Today people even speak about the necessity of evil and humanity's common bondage in guilt. This leads to consent to involvement in guilt. Ironically, people dismiss the world peace to which the prophets witness. They reject the elimination of government proclaimed in John's Revelation, and the transformation of the present social order through church community. They dismiss the communal life which has repeatedly been the self-evident expression of true love. The cynicism with which people try to dismiss these things shows that they no longer take a stand against evil. They avoid the decisive choice that Jesus represented: God or mammon.

People have turned away from the clarity of Jesus, who challenged us to say either yes or no and not something in between. People turn from the way of Jesus, weakly accepting a paradoxical situation in relation to God; all they can say in their vanity is "yes and no" or "no and yes" simultaneously. We must fight against this.

We were once challenged, "Surely you don't want to wage a general campaign against all evil?" Yes, this is exactly what it is all about. That is why Jesus came into the world. He called us and sent us out to take up this campaign against all evil in all things. He came to destroy the works of the devil. "God is light and in him there is no darkness."

■ Published as "Fort von Kompromiss und Schatten" in the periodical, *Wegwarte,* 1925, No. 10 / 11.

Against Bloodshed
and Violence

AGAIN AND AGAIN in the life of a nation, in the struggle for existence, and in the conflicts between nations, pent-up tensions erupt in violent outbursts. These outbursts reveal mutual exploitation and oppression and the savage instincts of covetous passion. This eruption of inordinate passions and merciless countermeasures has so intensified and spread that a decisive word is needed.

Some may see it as their task to uphold law and order by murderous means. Others may believe they are called to fight with bloodstained fists for the oppressed, for a future of justice and peace; others may regard their own race as holy and declare war on another race.

Our life as Christians has deeper roots. We have been entrusted with a task that looks further ahead. The mystery of life has been revealed to us because Christ means everything to us. We feel united with the entire church of Christ in which no group or individual can live isolated from the rest. They are members and organs of the one living body whose spirit, head, and heart is the coming Christ. The testimony of our life, therefore, is the essence of Christ's own life. He discloses to us the mystery of life when he points to the birds in the air and to the flowers in the meadow, and when he expects good fruits only from the healthy tree. He reveals to us the heart of the Father, who sends his rain and sunshine on the good and the bad.

Life means growth and development, the unfolding of love. Violence and coercion do not allow life to grow – they stifle it. We have been commissioned to serve life and build it up, no matter whether this seems evolutionary or revolutionary. The character of life rejects what is dying and awakens what is living to new life. This means development and upheaval. Yet no evolution, no upheaval, is able to eradicate the deepest root of world suffering: universal guilt, the poison of evil in hate, lust, depravity, and killing.

Organic life springs from God who is at work in all living things. It brings new birth. Every new beginning brings with it a separation, a painful liberation, a revolutionizing of the old. Yet every individual – indeed all of humankind – needs this new birth.

We believe in this new birth – a life of light from God. We believe in a future of love and constructive fellowship. We believe in the peace of God's kingdom, and that he will come to this earth. This faith does not mean we are imagining things only for the future – God will bring this future and give us his heart and spirit today. Christ lives in his church, which is the embodiment of his life. As the hidden, living seed of the future kingdom, the church has been entrusted with the peace that is characteristic of her and the love-spirit of the future. Therefore she shows herself in the present too, as justice, peace, and joy in this world.

No matter what its origin, we must speak up in protest against every instance of bloodshed and every power of violence and death. Our witness and will for peace, for love at any cost, even at the cost of our own lives, has never been more needed than it is today. Those who tell us that questions such as nonviolence, conscientious objection, and discipleship of Jesus are not relevant today are wrong. Today these questions are more relevant than ever. They will require perseverance in an absolute love that gives one the courage to die for one's beliefs.

Jesus knew he would never conquer the spirit of the world with more violence, but only by greater love. This is why he overcame the temptation to seize power over the kingdoms of this earth. What he proclaimed was God's rulership in the present and the future. God's will was present in his life, his words, his deeds, and his suffering. This is why in the Sermon on the Mount he speaks of those who are strong in love, the peacemakers, those with heart who will inherit the land and possess the earth. The kingdom of God belongs to them. He took up the ancient proclamation of peace and justice which belongs to the future kingdom of God. He deepened the crucial "Thou

shalt not kill" which ruled out all murder. He showed that
any cruelty – any brutal violation of the inner life – in-
jures body, soul, and, in fact, God himself, just as much as
killing the body.

It is regrettable that serious-minded Christians today
do not have the same clear witness of Jesus and of early
Christianity as was represented and proclaimed so
strongly in other centuries by living churches and movements. To them, war and the military profession were ir-
reconcilable with the calling of Christianity.

We do not deny the existence of radical evil and sin, nor
that the world will come to an end. But we do not believe
in the triumph of evil. We believe in God, the end of the
world as he wills it, the rebirth of the earth and humankind. This faith is not evolutionism, an inevitable ascent
to greater perfection. This faith believes in the growth
of the divine seed in consciences. It believes in the
Christ-spirit, in individual rebirth, in the fellowship of the
church. It also believes in an upheaval through world catastrophe. It sees war, revolution, and other horrors of the
end as part of the judgment and collapse of this depraved,
degenerate world of compulsion and coercion.

Faith expects everything from God alone. It is certain,
however, that God's seed and God's light is at work everywhere and that he reveals his heart and his future kingdom in his church, the church of Christ. True, the tension
between anti-Christian forces and the Christ-life is

present everywhere today, even in the Christian church. And it will become stronger, the more radically we in absolute love hold on to faith in what is to come. Faith is not afraid of the collision between the anti-Christian and Christ-centered spiritual forces. It expects and longs for this confrontation because the end has to come, and after it the completely new world.

It is an error to think that all Jesus wanted was to nourish the hungry soul. He concerned himself just as much with people's bodies as with their souls. Jesus also carried on, from John the Baptist and the Old Testament prophets, the proclamation of the future world order of peace and justice as surely and determinedly as he continued the proclamation of the rebirth of the individual.

Because we know there are many today who cannot respond to the language of the Old Testament – or who are not yet ready to do so – it is our task to spread the message of peace in whatever way we can. Hermann Hesse speaks with freshness and clarity on the commandment, "Thou shalt not kill":

> We are not yet men; we are still on our way to humanity. Every pupil of Lao-tse, every disciple of Jesus, every follower of Francis of Assisi was much further ahead than the laws and reasoning of present-day civilization. Yet the sentence, "Thou shalt not kill" has been honored faithfully and obeyed by thousands of people for thousands of years. There has always been a minority of well-meaning people

who had faith in the future, and obeyed laws which are not listed in any worldly code. As soldiers they showed compassion and respected their enemies, even during the last, horrible war, or consistently refused to kill and hate when ordered to do so, suffering imprisonment and torture as a result.

And we who believe in the future will raise the ancient demand again and again, "Thou shalt not kill." It is the basic demand of all progress, of all true humanity which is to come.

We kill at every step, not only in wars, riots, and executions. We kill when we close our eyes to poverty, suffering, and shame. For the consistent socialist all property is theft. In the same way all disrespect for life, all hardheartedness, all indifference, all contempt is, in the eyes of the believer, nothing else than killing. It is possible to kill not only what is in the present, but also what is in the future. With just a little skepticism we can kill a good deal of the future in a young person. Life is waiting everywhere. The future is flowering everywhere. We see only a small part of it and step on much of it with our feet. We kill with every step.

This is why every one of us has a personal task. This task is not to help all of humankind a little; it is not to improve some institution, not to abolish a particular kind of killing. All this is good and necessary, too. Yet the most important task for you and me is this: to take a step forward, in our own personal lives, from animal to human being.

■ Based on the article "Gegen Blut und Gewalt," published in *Das neue Werk* on April 15, 1921, to protest the widespread rioting in German cities. The quote from the German writer and poet Herman Hesse appeared in the magazine *Vivos Voco* in March 1919.

The Better Righteousness

I N THE SERMON ON THE MOUNT, Jesus shows us the character of his kingdom. It is imprinted on the citizens of the kingdom, who give it definite form. This character is built on a unique experience of God and brings a new ethic, a better justice.

The old morality, described by Jesus as the "righteousness of the scribes and Pharisees," is an outward righteousness, the product of legalism and of the coercion of society, church, and state. The better righteousness, in contrast, shows its nature as inner freedom. Independent of outward circumstances, this better righteousness allows nothing and no one to impose external directions on it. For this reason it opposes mammonistic servility. It builds upon God and on fellowship with him.

The comrades of the kingdom differ so sharply in character from everyone else that they can be compared only with the Father in heaven. "You, therefore, must be perfect, as your heavenly Father is perfect." God is the wellspring of life and overflowing love. We become his children and gain his character only by being reborn out of this spirit of the Father. Both the Sermon on the Mount and Jesus' talk with Nicodemus lead us into the mystery of community with God, the unity of the soul with God himself.

The only way to attain the new life of the Sermon on the Mount is through the fundamental experience which Paul calls liberation from the old man and the gift of the new man. Jesus himself is the new man, the second Adam, the life-giving spirit who leads us from the deadness of the old nature into the warm, powerful life of the new humanity. In fellowship with him we become the salt which overcomes the decay of death. In him we are the light, spreading a life-giving warmth and a clear vision. In him we gain the new nature whose life-core is God himself – the new nature of the spirit and of love.

The Sermon on the Mount emphasizes the relationship we should have to the Father when we pray. It gives us deep trust and confidence in the Father. Jesus is the door, the narrow gateway that leads us into fellowship with God. He frees us from vanity and arrogance, the underlying attitude of those who are pious and moral in their own strength. Face to face with Jesus we recognize our neediness, we become beggars before God. Therefore an essential mark of the new justice is a longing, a thirst for God that is unquenchable, a never-ending hunger for his righteousness.

This deep experience of the new life in God is a paradox: the awareness of utter neediness is combined with a clear decision and genuine single-mindedness. The righteousness of the moralist remains under pressure and compulsion, whereas the better righteousness of Jesus is spontaneous.

The deeds of this better righteousness come from a zest for life and innermost urge for action. Jesus' parable of the good tree and its good fruit, and of the rotten tree and its bad fruit, will always be vital in showing us how to distinguish the better justice from the old. Only those deeds that spring spontaneously from our inner nature should be regarded as good fruit. Our lives are lived within the better righteousness only when they bring forth this good fruit.

The better righteousness Jesus brings comes from the soul's encounter with God and reveals the Father's nature. Just as God cannot lie, the new justice is the simple truth that seeks genuine expression in everything. The moralistic attitude, the assertion of force and rights in the world, is now replaced by love which calls no halt – even in the face of the enemy.

This love comes to expression as a vital power to spread life and establish justice – a force so much stronger than all unhealthy, degenerate love. It demonstrates fidelity and purity of thought, and is a patient, merciful love, full of compassion for the whole world of suffering.

God's will is peace and justice. Only those who actually carry it out live in the sphere of the new kingdom. The

new life Jesus brings shows itself in deeds that work toward peace and justice for all people. We are deceiving
ourselves if we think that the old righteousness of standing on our rights is the wiser conduct. Jesus compares
anyone who does this to a foolish man whose house, built
on a poor foundation, must collapse. Only he who hears
and does Jesus' command can be compared to a wise man
who builds his house on a rock.

■ Published as "Die bessere Gerechtigkeit" in *Mitteilungen zur Förde-
rung einer deutschen christlichen Studentenbewegung* (News to Pro-
mote a Christian Student Movement in Germany), April 1919.

God or Mammon

J ESUS SAID, "No one can serve two masters; for either he will hate the one and love the other, or he will be devoted to the one and look down on the other. You cannot serve God and mammon."

The great and dynamic struggle that Jesus spoke of, "God or mammon," is still going on today. War has opened people's eyes to see that the pursuit of money, or preoccupation with outward things, is incompatible with all higher goals and purposes. *Mamona* was the Aramaic word for wealth, and it was in this wealth that Jesus saw the power of Satan. Even to Jesus himself Satan said, "I will give you all this if you will fall down and worship me." Devoting ourselves to a life of ease and pleasure means letting these outward things become the determining force in our lives. At the core of this service of mammon is the secret worship of things, a clinging to them and a love for them that amounts to a decision against God.

God and money are the two masters between whom one must choose, the two goals of living that cannot be reconciled. Already at the time of the early Christians, some scholars interpreted "Mammon" as a name of the devil Beelzebub. Others interpreted it as the name of a demon particularly connected with money in Satan's realm. Any attempt to combine service to God and service to mammon will end in failure. With one heart we must love God alone and cleave to him, despising mammon.

The materialistic view of life only makes demands for itself – wanting bodily ease, comfort, and pleasure. Anyone who values the easy life values material goods and is dominated by their power. He has been made a slave because he only wants to take; he has been deprived of that wealth of life in which one wants to give and bestow. The attitude of "What can life give me?" serves mammon and knows only rights and not responsibility. Its uppermost goal is payment and gain. We have to realize that most people, rich as well as poor, strive to secure property for their own benefit and comfort, often to the repression of everything else. So many are carried away by love for sensual happiness, comfort, and material pleasure. For believers, love of money is the old – and ever new – danger that threatened even the first Christians in the original church community.

Nothing but overcoming self will rid us of the false, debasing life that serves mammon. Even nonbelievers have recognized this. Zoroaster said, "Consume yourself in your own flame; how can you become new unless you first turn to ashes!" And Goethe wrote:

So long as thou hast not
This "die and live again,"
A gloomy guest thou art
Here on this dark earth.

BUT HOW IS IT POSSIBLE to "re-become," as the mystic
Eckhart expressed it; how can one "de-self oneself"(in
Goethe's words) when one is bound and fettered as
mammon's slave? How can one enter a strong man's house
and steal his goods, unless the strong man is bound first?
When a strong man guards his own dwelling his goods are
left in peace; but if someone stronger comes and conquers
him, the armor on which he relies is taken and the spoil
divided. Jesus is the stronger; he has overcome, disarmed,
and bound the enemy. It is the cross that triumphs over
the mammon-structure built by the devil. The victory of
the cross is deliverance from the sin of serving mammon,
from the deadness of a debased life. He died for all, so that
the living might no longer live for themselves but for him
who died for them and was raised. If we die with Christ,
we believe that we shall live with him. Therefore, "Set your
hearts on what is above, not on what is on earth. For you
have died, and your life is hidden with Christ in God."

■ Published as "Gott oder Mammon" in *Der Wahrheitszeuge* (The Witness to Truth), July 1915.

The Fight
Against Mammon

CHAPTER ELEVEN

I F LIFE IS LOVE and love means fellowship, if all living things interact to promote life and move together toward a future of unity and freedom, how is it possible that death, destruction, and murder are rampant in the world today?

Two powers are at work in the world: the one is the power of love, which leads people to fellowship with others; the other is death, which separates people and destroys the fellowship of love. This power poisons, making the organism of humanity sick and corrupt. It murders and kills. It isolates. It is egomania, the power of covetousness. This power radically attacks all that holds life together. It destroys the coherence of all living things. Alongside the constructive power and creative energy, the power that murders and enslaves is also at work.

Tension between opposites is a reality in our life today. When people try to consecrate their lives and want to devote themselves to a cause, or long for faith, they are faced with this either-or, God or mammon.

It is not true that everything religious is united and everything irreligious belongs to the other side. It would be nearer the truth to draw a dividing line right through both the religious and the nonreligious.

Not all relationships are connected to the same center, nor are they motivated by the same thing. The religion of many who call themselves Christians and confess to the name of Jesus Christ has nothing to do with the God of the Messiah or the coming kingdom. The question arises whether their religion is not really that of the Antigod; whether it is not permeated by the demonic powers of the abyss that cause the disintegration of humankind's solidarity. Is not the great world organization which names itself after Christ serving a god other than the God whom Jesus confessed, the God of a totally different order? Has not the institutional church sided with wealth and protected it, sanctified mammon, christened warships, and blessed soldiers going to war? Has not this church in essence denied him whom it confesses with words? Is the Christian state not the most ungodly institution that ever existed? Are not the state and the organized church, which protect privilege and wealth, diametrically opposed to what is to come: God's new order?

Does not reverence for church and state imply homage to Satan? Is not the justification of owning large property intrinsically worship of Satan? And hasn't this evil led to the apex of covetousness – the slaughter of fellow human beings? Wars arise only from the mammon spirit. Only out of the mammon spirit does prostitution arise. Can this devil possibly be identical with God and with Jesus Christ? You cannot serve God and mammon.

Early Christianity recognized in all sharpness that religiosity is hostile to God. The message that Christ's first witnesses brought was of the "transvaluation of all values," God's kingdom to come. They testified to a totally different order, calling it the message wrapped in mystery, concealed from those who are lost because they have been blinded by the god of this world.

The god of this world epoch, the interim god, stands opposed to the God who will set up the kingdom of Jesus Christ: justice, unity, and love. The former is the spirit of this world, personified by the media. This god of greed and murderous possessiveness is the spirit of the world. The first witnesses testified that we have not received the spirit of this world but the spirit that searches the depths of God, the spirit that nobody can know without being known by him.

NOBODY CAN SERVE two masters. "You cannot serve God and mammon." Jesus defined with utmost sharpness the nature of this mammon spirit. He unmasked the piety of the wealthy classes, exposing their worship of the spirit of death. This mammon spirit leads to war. It causes impurity to become business. Murder and lying become part of daily life because of this urge to possess.

Jesus called Satan the murderer from the beginning, the leader of unclean spirits. Murder is the nature of mammon. Wars are not the only sign of the mammon spirit. We have become used to countless people being crushed to death because of our affluence, as if they were vermin to be squashed.

Even the blind can see that the development of the mammon spirit means the incessant murder of hundreds and thousands of people. Mammon and big business rule through the power of the lying spirit. It is impossible to wage war without a basic inner deception. In the same way, only by lying and by duping the public can a capitalistic society be maintained.

This lie cannot be described, nor can we discuss it in detail here. It is up to each individual to examine the economic problems and to inquire into the murderous effects of the rule of mammon. If we were really concerned with the problem, if we saw how much injustice prevails without the world's conscience being aroused to action, we would realize the true situation very quickly. If people recognized that capitalism involves injustice, it would mean total revolt against the greatest deception in the history of mankind.

But we are a long way from revolting. Most pious circles and even working-class people think, "Rich and poor have to be. When a rich person can give work and livelihood to others, we have to be glad that such a one exists." This ignores the fact that it is impossible to amass this kind of fortune without cheating, without depriving and hurting others and destroying their lives. People fail to realize that big business, concentrated in a few hands, can push hundreds of thousands into certain ruin through unemployment. This is happening today.

Why do these facts remain hidden from us? How is it possible to be cheated of justice and be blind to it? It is because we ourselves are also under the rule of this god, mammon.

Mammon is the rule of money over people. Because we ourselves are dominated by the money spirit, we lack the strength to rebel. Dependence on material affluence and financial security – that is mammon. We recognize that money is the real enemy of God, but even so we are not in a position to apply the lever that lifts the slave rule of mammon off its hinges, because we are dependent on our income and our personal lives are broken by our own mammonism.

SPIRIT OR MONEY. God or mammon. Spirit is the deepest relationship, the innermost fellowship of everything that is alive. No one lives in isolation. All are interdependent, interrelated in groups, families, classes, trade unions, in nations, states, churches, and all kinds of associations. But not only this: through their humanity they are interrelated in a much deeper way. God gives us the richest relationships of love between people, from spirit to spirit, heart to heart, that lead to a growing, organic, constructive fellowship.

But there is a devilish means that seeks to rob all relationships of heart and spirit, of God. This means is money. Money reduces human relationships to a materialistic association, until the only value left is money itself. Satan uses property and money to destroy the highest goals. Eventually money becomes a commodity in itself instead of a means of barter, and this results in money as power. Many relationships are founded solely on finances, and people give up heart-to-heart relationships and let money transactions take their place. In the end, money destroys all true fellowship.

Money and love are mutually exclusive. Money is the opposite of love, just as sexual defilement of bodies is the opposite of love and respect; just as the killing in war is the radical opposite of life and of love that helps others; just as lying is the opposite of love and truth.

It would be impossible for capitalism to have such power to enslave and murder if the mammon spirit did not dominate. Where mammon rules, the possessive will is stronger than the will to community; the struggle to survive by mutual killing is stronger than the urge to love, stronger than the spirit of mutual help; destructive powers are stronger than constructive powers, matter is stronger than spirit, things and circumstances are stronger than

God, self-assertion stronger than the spirit of love and solidarity that brings fellowship. The spirit of mammon has never motivated people to work in a creative way for the life of fellowship. Instead it has engendered an enslavement of the soul and a scorn of it that has made us more subject to circumstances than religious people are to God. In truth, this spirit of mammon – the spirit of lying, impurity, and murder – is the spirit of weakness and death.

Jesus declared war on this spirit. He conquered it by overwhelming and healing its victims with his power. Jesus, the prince of life, declared himself the enemy of death. He lived among us to take away death's power and to destroy the devil's work. Christ's spirit of life overcomes death and brings fellowship among all living things. Christ was so conscious of this that he exclaimed, "Now the judgment of this world is come; now the prince of this world shall be cast out." The Spirit will convince people that this prince is defeated.

But now we have to ask how Jesus conducted this fight. Did he not say, "Make friends for yourselves through unjust mammon" and, "Therefore give back to Caesar the things that are Caesar's"? How can we reconcile this with these other words of his: "Do not lay up treasures on earth for yourselves! Woe to you who are rich! Woe to you who are full! And if someone sues you for your coat, give him your cloak as well"?

As soon as we follow Jesus we are ready to give up mammon, to declare war on it. When our inmost eye has been opened to his light, it no longer responds to what mammon demands. We can no longer accumulate property when our hearts are set on the new future, when we have the hope that God will establish a new kingdom. Then we shall turn our backs on everything else. We shall live for the future: freedom, unity, and peace for humanity. The saying, "Make friends for yourselves through unjust mammon" can be fulfilled when we give away property and wealth, gaining love and making friends who will be friends forever.

When that rich youth, who was not aware of having done anything wrong, came to Jesus, Jesus loved him at first sight. He asked him whether he loved God and his neighbor. The youth thought he had done as he ought in every way. "Good," said Jesus, "If this is really so, then you must now make this love real. Go and sell everything, give it to the poor, and come with me."

The god Jesus met when he entered the temple was not his God, but the god mammon: cattle and cattle dealers, banks and bankers. Jesus made a whip, not to strike people in the face but to turn over the tables and show his contempt for money. He testified that this house should belong to God, not to mammon. When a spy came and showed him a piece of money, the coin of the emperor, he answered, "Give to Caesar what belongs to Caesar and to God what belongs to God."

When someone was needed to manage the common purse on the long journeys, Judas was asked to be the keeper: Judas, who Jesus knew would become the betrayer. The murderer from the beginning was exposed in the very midst of Jesus' disciples, and he ended where murder must end. Judas betrayed the secret: that Jesus knew he was the Messiah-King of the new order. Jesus then stood his ground when questioned by the political and religious authorities, "Are you the Messiah, the Son of the highest?" He answered, "I am; you shall see the Son of Man seated at the right hand of Power, and coming on the clouds of heaven to establish his kingdom." They put him to death because of this revolutionary confession.

This attack on the order of mammon seemed to spell the end of the spirit-born community: its leader was killed. The power of money seemed to triumph in religious and irreligious alike; the will of mammon and death seemed to have the upper hand.

Yet through the very execution of the leader of this new order, through the grave itself, life had the final victory. Some men and women of the downtrodden Jewish people met to wait for something completely new. They waited for the Spirit. They knew that this spirit of love, of order, of freedom was the spirit of God's kingdom. And the

Spirit came upon them, bringing about a church, a fellowship of work and goods in which everything belonged to all, and in which all were active to the full extent of their powers and gifts.

Yet this church, too, succumbed to the deadly process that destroys life. Just as individuals die, so this church also died. But in the course of the centuries a new church rose. Time and again small communities were formed in which men and women declared war on mammon and took upon themselves a poverty that was filled with generosity. In actual fact, in choosing this poverty they chose the richest way. People filled with an urge to love can be found throughout the centuries. We hear their voices and we join hands and feel a fellowship of faith with them, faith in the future.

God has demonstrated that he did not die; but the mammon spirit shows that it too is at work. God is waging a crucial war against death and mammon. The God of Jesus Christ is not yet God over all things. He is the God who is on the way, who lives when his kingdom breaks in, the goal of all goals. He is the end where everything meets. He is the protest against death and murder, a rebuke to everything in us that lusts and robs and grasps. He is the conqueror who clears out the robbers' den and judges all who covet possessions and property. Throughout history he has revolted against perverted humankind.

Simple communism existed among primitive peoples. And throughout history the revolutionary struggle, the fight against materialism, continued as a vital issue. We who see the appalling results of capitalism today stand at the point where the uprising against capitalism begins. We are on the same side as all revolutionaries who fight against mammon. "He who is not against me is on my side. He who is not on my side is against me." These words of Jesus hold true for us.

There are two ways, both committed to the fight against mammon. One way holds the ideals of socialism and communism. The other is the new way of communal work and fellowship in things spiritual and material – the voluntary gathering of those who are free of private property and capital. This is the organic growth of the seed that sprouts in a stony field. Here and there a little tip of grass shows. After a few days have passed and sun and rain have touched these shoots, you can see a field of living green. A few weeks later you will see a whole field of flourishing life. In spite of weeds and stones, the young crop breaks through. What the individual blade of grass cannot achieve, the whole field can. The harvest is there! Pray that laborers may be sent out into the harvest.

Wheat and weeds cannot be separated before the harvest. We must wait for harvest time, otherwise wheat is torn out and grass left standing. It would be completely contrary to the spirit of Jesus to hang the servants of mammon on lampposts in a bloody revolution, so that only people of the community spirit were left. There are still covetous people who will say, "Now it is our turn to take away the rights of others." We cannot put our trust in such words; they lack the spirit we witness to through Christ.

We can have no part in violent revolution, because it allies itself with the father of lies and brings about bloodshed. It is self-deception to think we can overcome mammon by physical violence, for violence is the same evil spirit as mammon. We cannot drive out poison by means of poison. The new can be born only of the new; only out of life comes life; only of love can love be born. Only out of the will to community can community arise.

Community is alive where small bands of people meet, ready to be merged in the one goal and belong to the one future. Already now we can live in the power of the future; already now we can shape our lives in accordance with God and his future kingdom. The victory of the Spirit is proved in the church community. The kingdom of love, which is free of mammon, is drawing very near. Change your thinking radically so that you will be ready for the coming order.

Now listen, you rich people, weep and wail because of the misery that is coming upon you. Your wealth has rotted, and moths have eaten your clothes. Your gold and silver are corroded. Their corrosion will testify against you and eat your flesh like fire. You have hoarded wealth in the last days. Look! The wages you failed to pay the workmen who mowed your fields are crying out against you. The cries of the harvesters have reached the ears of the Lord Almighty. You have lived on earth in luxury and self-indulgence. You have fattened yourselves in the day of slaughter. You have condemned and murdered innocent men who were not opposing you.

Be patient, then, my brothers, until the Lord's coming (James. 5:1–7).

■ "The Fight Against Mammon," "Mammon and the Living God," and "The Decision" are three lectures, all bearing originally the same title, "Der Gott Mammon" and given October–December 1923 and January 1924.

Mammon and
the Living God

THE PERSIAN PROPHET ZOROASTER gave a threefold message as a guide to true life on earth: truth, purity, and work on the land. This thinker recognized, however, that other forces opposed the tremendous power of truth, purity, work, and the fellowship of love arising out of this trinity. He realized that two opposing powers were active in this world. Zoroaster was the first prophet outside Judaic prophecy to express this so strongly, but the two opposing powers he speaks of are not inseparably divided, such as this world and the other world, or spirit and matter. Rather, he saw these powers as two opposing poles challenging each other: good and evil, life and death, light and darkness, obscurity and clarity, the contrast between day and night. He wanted to expose the struggle between good and evil in this world.

Every evening when the sun sets; every night as it grows dark and the moon rises to conquer the deep blue-blackness of the starry heavens; every morning when the morning star rises to herald the coming of the sun and a new day is born of the night, we see a symbol of the birth and death of light. The moon, which wanes and then becomes radiant and full again, belongs to this cycle. All point to a mystery – the marvelous victory of light over darkness, of good over evil.

Zoroaster put it beautifully:

God creates spirit,
spirit creates truth,
truth gives freedom,
freedom gives faith.
God says: I will be with you.
And there are you,
born of selfishness,
spirits of evil
and the prophets thereof,
and thou the first among them –
glittering lies!
Your deeds are the same;
they are known
in all the earth's regions.
You have your power
by flattering people,
lulling them by things pleasant,
so they tire of working on themselves
and stagger away
from God and from their duty.

You call this life?
Of true life this is death!
With your worldliness

you rob people of eternity.
But this is what evil wants;
it wants annihilation.
On a thousand ways it lurks;
thou alone, God, knowest them all.
The better and the evil shall end;
then what was good shall emerge.
Even the wisest among us
cannot judge.
Even the holiest
has his sins.
God alone knows what is right.

I only know
that something in my heart
is smothered by the teachings of these;
that the longing for goodness
is gradually choked,
and that I cry for redemption.
Therefore I call him a false teacher
who defames what is deepest for me,
who corrupts my earth for me,
and hinders me from looking
up to heaven;
who makes the clever merely cunning,
teaching them but temporal gain,
and striking down him who wants more.
Yet they themselves
live on the want of others,

cheating men of their wages,
and by their actions
misleading more and more others
to do likewise.
Did not all the prophets
speak from hearts as troubled as mine?
Did not the same anger
flare up in them
against the horde
that denied the earth – open to all –
to others, by laws and verdicts,
as by a sorcerous spell?
Make the earth free again for us;
it is the victim of madmen now.
Clergy and nobility hem life in,
but with life we shall triumph.
For our life is more
than eating and drinking;
it is justice,
and justice prevails
throughout heaven and earth.
From God we draw our strength;
who will stand against us?
Lord, give me strength in my efforts;
do not forsake me! Thou knowest
that I cry out like this
only because I love people.

Yet behold, a din
of voices arises,
a chaos of sound.
There are those who remember
their loyalty to thee;
they cling to thee and call out to thee.
The others forget what thou gavest;
they leave thee and cry treason.
But to those who still waver,
thoughts move from one to the other,
speaking in secrecy.

But alas, Lord,
I am in the midst of them.
Therefore I ask thee:
How is it to be,
now and for all the future?
Is the good which is done
and the evil which happens
written down as in a book
for a final reckoning?

This I ask thee:
How shall it not be forgotten
that the wicked are helped
to do violence;
that people feed themselves
by pillaging others,
animals, and the land?

This I ask thee:
whether in goodness there really is
a possibility of action;
whether cunning is not the thing
that really counts in this world?
Yes, O my God,
does this not seem the only way
to reach the goal?
At sight of this world
I want to cry out:
Can it really be that truth is the better,
when there is so much lying;
and must I not join
in their howling?

God, do not forsake me.
Make me strong in this trial.
Give me strength.
Down with thee, O rebellious thought;
the sword at thy throat!
For look well:
Does this bring inward peace
over home and community,
over country and world?
Is the deepest life healed
by craving for outward things?
Only those who know

from which source life springs
can draw from the eternal well,
and only this refreshment is true comfort.
Sparks once flew,
and there will be flame again:
the better and the evil,
two sticks that rub each other;
but the fire is good, only good!

Step here or there,
be smoke or flame,
be crushed, suffocating in smoke,
be raised in flames!
There you are, yours is the choice!
But know that you do not choose
between God and the evil one.
As long as you still have to choose
you know nothing of him yet.
For God is higher and deeper.
He gives constantly
a world that never perishes,
the secure peace of truth,
the peace of his spirit.

WHOEVER FOLLOWS these ancient words will feel what a tremendous struggle comes to expression here. Any superficial distinction between people becomes impossible.

There are many who believe that religious people, the idealists, the devout, are on one side in this struggle, while materialists, those concerned with outward things, are on the other side. Certainly, this classification has a certain justification, but it does not go to the bottom of the matter. Basically, it misses the point.

The great struggle takes place in the heart of every person – in every materialist just as much as in every idealist or religious person. We cannot say that the good are on one side and the bad on the other. It is not true that the religious life is good and the materialistic life is bad. The important thing is to discern where materialistic thinking puts its faith, and where religious life finds its god – where the spirit of each is found and what it values.

IN RELIGION AS WELL as in atheism there is an Antigod whom we can worship. The early Christians were convinced that there is a god in the world who is not the God of Jesus Christ. There is a god of godless, worldly religion, antagonistic to the life of Jesus; a god of the present era, hostile to God's future and his eternity.

The nature of the Antigod is work without soul, business without love, machinery without spirit, and lust instead of joy. It craves for possessions without mutual help, destroys competitors and idolizes private property, obtained through fraud. This god is not the God of goodness. He is not the God of love. He is not the God of community or of the future; not the Father of Jesus, nor the One who will bring the coming order of justice. No, he is a god of the present age, an interim god. A god of the abyss, a fiend of darkness with the power to corrupt everything and bring death.

This mighty demon of our age cannot simply be equated with superstition, yet superstition is part of it. Superstitious beliefs hold to the power of numbers and days, and fear the demonic power of influential areas of life. This power extends beyond these spheres, compelling soldiers to wear an amulet around their necks so that while murdering they will not be murdered themselves. People try to exorcise evil spirits by means of charms, not realizing that they themselves are possessed by these spirits. This demonic, evil power operates even in the most religious places where religion puts on its most pious mask.

We read in early Christian writings that a god of this world has blinded the minds of those who cannot believe and are perishing. It has corrupted their vision so that they are no longer able to see what really matters or to grasp the message of the future, the message of liberation, of mankind's coming unity, of the coming God. Because the spirit of this world is not of God, it cannot see the purity and truth of his future or recognize the deep things of God. Rather, it seeks to explore all vices and passions and is concerned with the things of Satan. It seeks friendship with death and its weapons and wants to know evil by actually experiencing it. This spirit paralyzes and intoxicates, giving an illusion of power, while only weakening. Jesus laid his hand upon a woman suffering a disease that bent her body and made her utterly weak. Jesus said of this woman that Satan had bound her and she had to be set free.

This spirit of darkness is the spirit of weakness, disintegration, and death. We all know the effects of this spirit from personal experience. Liberation from this spirit deepens our awareness of its deadly atmosphere. An early Christian writing says: "We were dead in our trespasses, going along with this world epoch, with the prince who rules our atmosphere, with the spirit that is now at work in the people of disobedience." Not until the spell begins to break do we recognize how powerfully this spirit had us in its grip.

We are so closely bound up with this spirit of death that we become incapable of discerning its dangerous nature. We do not have the perspective to recognize its character clearly. Therefore we need a serene and pure spirit of truth to lead us in discerning the nature of this spirit of our age.

This spirit is the spirit of fashion, not only the fashion of the moment but the fashion of our entire epoch. It will only be unmasked and overcome when the new era puts an end to it.

But the resplendent star of the coming day has risen:

Jesus, the leader of the coming age, declared war on this spirit. Victory presupposes warfare, the clear demarcation of the enemy's front lines. Jesus spoke of this fight and of certain victory when he said, "You cannot serve two masters. You cannot serve God and mammon." The ancient Persian Zoroaster and all the Jewish prophets foretold the battle that Jesus was to inaugurate. With many colors they painted their glowing optimism for the victory of good over evil.

WE WOULD NOT be able to understand the words "the god mammon" unless we knew the other terms by which Jesus exposes this spirit. He calls it the murderer from the beginning, the father of lies, the unclean spirit. Its nature is materialism, its trade is murder, its character lying, its countenance impurity. To the moralist, these four traits are unrelated, but for those with more insight there is no fundamental difference. Mammonism is the covetous will – to seize, possess, and enjoy. It destroys other lives for the sake of ownership and gratification by suggesting that another's life is obstructing one's own possession and pleasure, or by inducing the intoxication of lust. The Hedonists enhance their own existence and increase their own power while corrupting the lives of others. The covetous will that governs mammon makes them twofold murderers. Lying, cowardice, and immorality are the consequences of the same covetous will. Anyone possessed by the covetous, murderous spirit of mammon and unbridled sexual lust will have to tell lies.

In business, lying hides the greed of mammon, the selfishness of human efforts, and the materialism behind relationships. People in business are forced to appear different from what they are, for nobody wants to associate with a beast of prey or a hyena that lives on carcasses. So the ravenous wolf has to don the white fleece of the lamb; the sly hyena has to put on the mask of the honorable citizen, and the old fox has to feign innocence. Business fraud and deception has to be carried out as inoffensively as possible.

Lying and deceit are part of all warfare between nations and social classes. For the weapons of truth and clarity cannot possibly be used to defend greed and selfishness. This dishonest state of affairs shows that trust, unselfishness, and dedication to the global community are required in all areas of life. If human society is to survive, ethical and altruistic motives must at least be simulated. And these motives, morally sound though they may be, are fragile and, more often than not, mixed with the drive for power and the craving for pleasure.

This is the only explanation for the "honest" appearance of the businessman who destroys competitors and takes advantage of his clients. It is the only rationale for the "high" morals behind destruction in wars, including civil wars; for ruthless acts of state that deliberately dispossess and harm other nations. It explains the patronizing exploitation, the oppression and starving of workers by their employers. For the perceptive person, this lying makes a clear case for the truth it simulates.

The same is true of the deceitfulness of impurity that arises from the abyss of covetousness. Unfaithfulness in sex relations is the profoundest and meanest deception imaginable. It kills the soul by deceit and trickery. Nowhere is there so much lying as in "love," where real love is feigned for the sake of abuse and gratification without restraint.

All this shows clearly that these apparently different designations – mammon, lying, murder, and impurity – disclose one and the same spirit, one and the same "god." The reality around us shows the enormous power this god possesses in the world. We will be more and more alarmed by Jesus' words summoning us to battle: No man can serve two masters. You cannot serve God and mammon. This has great significance: lay up no treasure for yourself on earth. Sell all you have and give to the poor, and come, and go a totally new way with me.

It seems impossible to break these chains. Wealth works as a curse because it stands in the way of liberation. It is an affliction because it burdens and satiates but cannot fulfill. Property kills friendship and gives rise to injustice. Woe to you that are rich, woe to you that are full. Blessed are you that are poor. There has to be a great turning point, when true friendship will be won by giving away property, when fellowship will be found by turning away from injustice. Make friends for yourselves through unjust mammon. Win hearts by giving away all you own. Go the new way of fellowship and community given by the Spirit; seek the unity that comes from God and penetrates through the soul into material things. Flee from mammon and turn to God!

ON HEARING THE WORD "mammon" we think of money first of all. And indeed money is the most tangible symbol of mammonism. Mammon means valuing wealth and converting human relationships into material values.

People live in relationship to one another. The child is born from the mother; and father, mother, brothers, and sisters all guide the child into life. At school a child continues to grow, surrounded by the companionship of classmates. Later, the young person starts to work and gets to know coworkers. In this process he gains an understanding for a life where people work together and serve each other.

Love enters the life of the young person. Two people become one in joy and faithfulness, sharing life and possessions. In them and through them the tremendous reality and coming-into-being of life community begins its new cycle.

Just as in an individual life, so in the life of the social classes and nations nothing exists alone. No age, no century, not even an instant in time stands by itself; everything is interrelated. The more living these relationships, the fuller and richer is life.

Naturally, this relationship can also be one of opposition, even of strife. Strife, too, is a relationship. Sometimes the honest adversary is a better friend, because we can come closer to another heart through an open disagreement than through an indifferent or superficial relationship.

"Love your enemies" is not only an enormous demand: it powerfully embraces and affirms the lives closest to us. Except for my friends, my enemies are closest to me. It is with them that I have to come to terms most frequently in my thoughts and actions – most of all in my inner feelings. It is to my enemies, no less than my friends, that I have to show the strength of my heart. Since I cannot avoid this, the question is: in what spirit will this be most fruitful? What will yield the most living relationship? The only way is love. Only then will my relationship to my enemies be fruitful. The German poet Schiller said, "When I hate, I rob myself of something; but when I love I become richer by the object of my love."

Life is relationship, interaction, giving and receiving,

coming and going, and daily working side by side. People are called to fellowship of emotion and will, of knowledge and creative work, of faith and hope. They are called to a fellowship of life!

But here is money – the mightiest power in the present world system – that stifles and obstructs this fellowship. Everything that would otherwise be a living interchange, a service of mutual help, becomes a dead coin, a piece of paper. Money in itself is not evil, but the way it swallows up what is living in man's spirit is evil. This, then, is the satanic nature of money: we have financial relationships that are no longer personal, no longer part of a fellowship of faith and life.

Our civilization knows no fellowship; people buy and pay for each other. Because of money, people are no longer valued as human beings but as a commodity, and work is paid for and consumed. It is not surprising, therefore, that in trade there is even less of a relationship between those who produce and sell the goods and those who receive them. People consume the goods they have paid for without any care about the people who produced them.

Money contains all the work and effort of people whom we neither know nor care about. It makes people forget the mutual exchange that takes place in work done and services rendered. Our relationships become materialistic, converting the spirit of fellowship into its opposite. From this results the soul-killing practice of receiving payment for services, of employing for labor, without any community between the receiver and the giver. Wherever and whenever this happens we have fallen prey to mammon, to Satan. All these business and labor relationships, impersonal and devoid of spirit, are built on money.

Today it is almost impossible for an employer in a factory to have contact with the workers and to care about them personally, though in terms of money he has a clearly defined relationship. For the shareholders in a corporation, this is even less likely. The mutual relationship between the investors and those who do the work has been eliminated by the shareholders, the company, the board of directors, and the management, all pushed between investor and worker. No one is personally responsible for what happens to the worker. The shareholder can defer to the board of directors, and the board of directors can defer to the investors. There is no way for the working masses to establish a relationship with their employers. It has been displaced by the inaccessible stock company and its drive for efficiency.

This is why the soul has been trampled on in modern industry and business, where money, accounts, and payroll statistics are first priorities. The worker counts only as a payroll number, a profit statistic. Everything personal, everything that creates fellowship, has been eliminated from the process of production. This is characteristic of the machine and the system it creates. The soul is not admitted into the factory. It is handed over at the time clock. In return the worker receives a number from the time clock and has to function as part of the huge machine, where instruments enforce the production schedule.

THERE ARE COUNTLESS examples in all spheres of life where money and profit kill the soul and make fellowship in work impossible. Money – originally intended as a means of exchange – has turned into accursed mammon and has become the all-subduing power agent. It works through covetousness, judges things by their monetary value, and devaluates the soul.

This makes a man like Francis of Assisi, with his voluntary poverty and rejection of money, so needed in our capitalistic era. People often react with indignation to those who refuse to touch money for the sake of love and freedom. Yet this reaction shows that the deluding power of money can be abolished by a single step into the economically impossible. In the end, money or elimination of money are only symbols for what is real and essential.

Mammon is not merely the same as money or private property, though it is true that all of these are overcome by the Spirit. The God of the coming kingdom of love is not found simply by doing without money or by having common property. Mammon is in communism as well as in capitalism. For many dispossessed, the need for food, clothing, and housing is the force that drives them. In the struggle for existence, the war of the have-nots against the haves is waged to the end. Our whole life is a material one and arises automatically out of the instincts of self-preservation and reproduction. This way of thinking is still mammonism. For if we build our mutual relationships only on the requirements of food, clothing, shelter, and sex, then we base these relationships on a materializing of the spirit.

THERE IS A GREAT and deep truth in the protest that arises from Marxism. This movement for social justice does not primarily strive for materialism or the economic interpretation of history; nor are they after "surplus value" (the difference between wages paid to a worker and the value of his work). They do not strive for an easy transition from capitalism to a socialist state enterprise via trusts, and certainly not for collective economy as such. No, the driving force of this movement is faith in the ultimate future of justice, faith in the victory of light and in a fellowship that will extend to material things, embracing everything. The hidden force behind this materialism is the revolt of the spirit in the name of matter; it is a mass attack on the mammonism of those "spiritual" people who have the spirit on their lips but materialism in their minds.

Moreover, the materializing of relationships through

money can be overcome – in the upper classes too – by uniting hearts in brotherliness and administering goods justly for the benefit of all. Faith in an ultimate future of justice can be alive among capitalists; it can be alive in materialistic socialists; for it can live in the heart that seeks love and believes in a just future. If we feel this, then we can be convinced – like Zoroaster – that there is a power of good, which is stronger, at all times and in all places, than the force of mammonism.

In our world this faith seems impossible. What shakes us deeply in Zoroaster's verses is that even he doubted whether, after all, evil and cunning would not finally gain the upper hand. But again and again he fights through to the faith that the spirit with the greatest power must triumph. The greatest power is the light, which is truth and purity and active dedication. The greatest power is love.

THE CERTAINTY OF LOVE is the hope of early Christianity and the Old Testament. God is creative power; he is love and truth and clarity. He has a goal which will mean justice and peace on this earth. This God is the God of the future, and he will bring the victory of truth and purity over lying and impurity, the victory of the creative spirit of justice and love over unjust mammon.

Mammonism exterminates the fellowship of life. It is death, the enemy of life. Jesus took up the fight against the spirit of mammon in the certainty that he would triumph. But we must get rid of the idea that the kingdom Jesus proclaimed is purely otherworldly, that his intention was to make good one day in heaven everything that is bad on earth. We would have to become people of the other world, who long above all for the hour of death – people like those monks who lie in their coffins every day to be prepared for death. To die would be man's liberation. Death would be the redeemer, giving us the final kiss to freedom from the shackles of this shameful existence. Then by death we would be lifted out of the accursed bodily life into a paradise of spirits, a paradise of pure, ethereal joys.

But the kiss of death is not the kiss of the liberator. It is the poisonous breath of the ravager. Whatever leads to death, whatever pushes people out of life and the living fellowship of mutual dedication, whatever ruins health and beauty in life, is of the devil. Death is the last enemy to be conquered.

What was said for Zoroaster must be said just as strongly for Christ. The great division between God and the devil is not the division between life here and life beyond, between matter and spirit, between corporeality and incorporeality – it runs right through all spirits and all bodies, through all eternities and all times. In every house both spirits are at work in full force. In every body, every human being, both powers are at work. Both forces operate in every age, in every moment of history, including this one now.

The decisive question is: how will the spirit of life come to rule in each person, in each moment, in each body, and throughout the whole planet earth? And how will mammon, the world spirit of covetousness and injustice, be conquered and eliminated?

BROTHERS AND SISTERS, love the earth. Brothers and sisters, be true to the earth, and do not believe those seducers who look longingly to the world beyond, casting suspicion on this world. Jesus is the greatest friend of the earth – Jesus who again and again, in the original spirit of Judaism, proclaimed love for this earth, love for the soil, love for the land. Blessed are the peacemakers, for they shall possess the earth.

In Zoroaster's writing we find the combination of truth, purity, and work on the land as the basic promise for divine life. In Jesus and the prophets of Judaism, the proclamation of God's coming kingdom testifies to the same miracle of "spirit and land." God, the spirit of love and justice, purity and truth, will come; his creative rulership will burst in upon this earth and bring the new time. This earth shall become a garden of justice, truth, and purity of mutual relationships. Then the God-ordained joy of life will begin on this planet. The earth shall be conquered for a new kingdom, a new order, a new unity, a new joy in true community.

Jesus brings the message today, and we must believe it and live in accordance with it: seek first the kingdom of the new order of God. Seek God's future, God's coming. All other things on which the spirit of mammon wants to build up life should not concern you. What matters is the new order that transforms and recreates everything. The means for your daily life will be given at the right time. When you are born anew by God, you will tread underfoot the devil of mammon, murder, lying, and impurity. As a free person you will stride into the new life. Already now you must proclaim and live in the new kingdom.

It is not a matter of a future utopia in some far-off place. On the contrary, the certainty of this future is a present power. God, who brings the future onto this earth, is alive today, and his spirit will unite all people. Whoever believes in his coming and in the victory of his spirit – whoever believes in Christ – can know his power and can make the decision of faith here and now, renouncing unjust mammon. This person will let the covetous will die, will stop telling lies and taking part in murderous acts, and will stop craving what is impure.

This is the secret of the fellowship of faith – it is happy in love without being covetous in lust. The mystery of this expectation is that it puts into action the love for all people, in the simplest work on the land – in field and garden – and in manual or mental work.

The same divine spark lives in every human being. The poet Schiller, in his *Ode to Joy,* writes jubilantly of the brotherly love that embraces the millions in the world. From the starry firmament, from the Father of love, the spirit of the future is bestowed; it gives eternal life to the love that fulfills life by sacrificing itself in devoted work for others. It is a simple thing: joy in everything that lives. Anyone who can rejoice in life, in other people, in the fellowship of church community – anyone who feels joy in the mutual relationships of trust and inner fellowship – such a person experiences what love is. Anyone who cannot feel joy cannot live.

Love is born of joy. Only where there is joy do love and justice dwell. We need the spirit of joy to overcome the gloomy spirit of covetousness, the spirit of unjust mammon and its deadly hate. We can only have such joy if we have faith, and if we believe that the earth has a future. The great hope that is ultimate certainty must arise anew.

ONCE DURING A MEETING of socialists, independents, and communists, the leaders challenged the exhausted workers to close ranks for the solidarity of their union. We asked these leaders and the whole assembly, "What is the use of calling for solidarity among workers? What is the purpose of challenging them to have courage for a united action and to gather strength after a total defeat if they have no faith in the future? Do they believe that there can be a just distribution of the necessities of life, and that a just and peaceful fellowship of work is possible? Only if this faith is living will there be solidarity. If it is not, there will be none. Is this faith still alive?" They all had to admit that this was the crucial question. Certainly, they felt that this faith had been weakened among the workers – but even so it could not be entirely destroyed. All were unanimous that this faith could not die.

However sharply they stress their differences, there is one thing that should unite political factions, Christians and non-Christians: the inner certainty that everything must be completely different, that what destroys fellowship and shatters trust must be overcome. In its place the joy of love, the fellowship of justice, will be victorious.

This faith is not purely spiritual; it is ultimate reality. It comes from God, the source of all reality, who himself is creative life. This faith is the certainty that mammon with all its evils will be overcome by the loving, living God.

The distribution of land, work, and goods should be in harmony with the justice of God, who lets the sun shine and the rain fall on the just and the unjust. Jesus says simply: what you want people to do for you, do for them. Make sure that all others have what you think you need yourself.

Let us unite. Let us go to all people, so that together we have community in all things. To become real people we must become brothers and sisters! To be brothers and sisters we must be real people. To become a community we must be alive. There is one living fellowship – brotherhood through faith. There is one faith – the faith that believes in everything that overcomes death, faith in the living God.

■ See note for "The Fight Against Mammon," chapter 11.

The Decision

A DANGEROUS AND WIDESPREAD ERROR is the belief that everything religious comes from God, the Father of our Lord Jesus Christ. Jesus and the apostles of the early church discerned connections and opened up abysses of which most people who call themselves Christians have no inkling.

The apostles declared that there is a god of this world that is completely different from the living God. They spoke of a spirit that rules and possesses this world. This god creates confusion in the hearts of unbelievers, blinding their senses so that they cannot perceive the gospel, the true message from God and his Son. A contemporary drama portrays this spirit as the devil of sensuality. Much that we call Christian is anti-Christian; what we call divine is anti-divine; what we call religious comes from this other spirit that is opposed to God.

Jesus unmasked the nature of the god of this world. He calls him the father of lies, the murderer from the beginning; he calls him mammon and the spirit of impurity. He shows how sharply the prince of this world is opposed to God the Father. The devil desperately tries to keep this truth hidden. He is not the father of Jesus, who is the

truth; he is the father of lies. It is important for us to recognize that, wherever lies dominate, religious falsehood
prevails, which has nothing to do with Jesus and his God
but with the god of this world, with Satan and the spirit
that controls the children of unbelief.

Lying in any form comes from below, and most terrify-
ing of all is the religious lie, which is always closely tied to
people's disposition to murder. It discloses the nature of
hell. Think of the two World Wars and the media during
the wars; or think of the revolutionary struggles and the
news of that time, and you will see that everywhere the
lying spirit and murder are bound to one another. Every
spirit that is out to kill comes from the devil. Every spirit
that untruthfully belittles the opponent, that is silent
about the good in his nature and exaggerates the bad,
comes from below.

All wars and revolutions have proven that sexual impurity and unfaithfulness are inseparably bound to lying
and the spirit of murder and crime. I am constantly aware
of this through tragic experiences with people I have
come to know. I know an army officer who is a devastated
man, close to madness. He did not know how to break
with his mistress and was in constant fear of this woman
who shared his guilt in what they had done: an abortion
was intended to prevent further trouble and disclosure.
But she could betray him at any time and ruin him. Be-

cause of the murder of unborn life which he had on his conscience, he felt forced to drag along the unbearable burden of his impure life. Fear of punishment and public prosecution forced him to continue in this lying life, until he was a ruined man.

These three terrible forces of hell – lying, impurity, and murder – which generate such a sinister power in our age, are combined with a fourth power, commonly over-looked: the spirit of mammon.

Without the spirit of mammon there would be no war. In the grip of this spirit, love can be purchased and bodies thrown into the gutter and corrupted. Because of the mammon spirit, lying is carried to extremes – the lying people do to each other in business, in relationships be-tween the classes, and in the dialogue between the na-tions. "You cannot serve God and mammon." Making life dependent on financial circumstances, mammon gains control and overrides all other relationships.

People never live alone, but always in groups, families, tribes, and nations – ultimately as one great fellowship on this earth. Between these human beings there exist mani-fold relationships created by God – heart-to-heart rela-tionships of love, leading to the organic building up of community. However, where property and money are the deciding factors, the personal relationships are broken up in diabolical ways.

Money materializes men's relationships to one another. It has grown from a means of barter to a commodity, a possession in itself. It has gained in importance because people need to interact but do not want to come too close to one another, because they are afraid of a genuine relationship.

The spirit of mammon controls people by things instead of by the spirit of love, and depends on circumstances and conditions instead of on God. It hardens the heart in egoism, the product of self-love, which is the opposite of the spirit that lives for others and gives itself for others.

We realize, then, that it is impossible to serve God and mammon at the same time. It is an either-or decision. Either we are dependent on God and love him and become people of love, with a sincere contact with others, overcoming all disposition to murder or to injure another's livelihood, and remaining free of the filthy impurity that drags love into the dirt. Or we are people of mammon, and in our relationships consider how much money we earn, what advantages we have, how we can be financially successful and amass more money. This hardens our hearts and destroys our longing for God. As a result the deepest urges of love in our own hearts become corrupted, including love of man for woman and woman for man.

This great decision, then, is the ultimate decision in each person's life. It is the decision between hell and heaven, between the Creator in his Holy Spirit of love and the degenerate creature in his final corruption. It is the decision between God and devil.

ONCE A WEALTHY young man came to Jesus. Jesus saw so much longing for the good and pure in him that he loved him at first sight. He was in fact a man of noble traditions and trustworthy morals, who wanted to learn from Jesus. So he asked Jesus, "Teacher, what good things shall I do so that I may have eternal life?" After he claimed that he had killed no one, never committed adultery, never stolen or given false witness; yes, after claiming that he honored father and mother and loved his neighbor as himself, Jesus pointed out to him the untruthfulness of his claim: he had not loved his neighbor as himself. Jesus said to him, "If you want to be perfect, go and sell what you possess, give it to the poor, and you will have treasure in heaven. Come and follow me." When the young man heard this he went away sorrowful, for he had many possessions. And Jesus said to his disciples, "Truly, I tell you, a rich man will find it hard to enter the kingdom of heaven. I also tell you, it is easier for a camel to go through the eye of a needle than for a rich man to enter God's kingdom." When his disciples heard this they were astonished and said, "Then who can be saved?" But Jesus looked at them and said, "With men this is impossible, but with God all things are possible."

The rich youth believed that he loved his neighbor as himself, but Jesus wanted to lead him deeper, to show him whether it was true that he loved his neighbor as himself. The youth valued his property and the ease and comfort of his outward existence. Now the Lord said to him, "First love your neighbor as yourself, then I will tell you how you can be perfect. If you love your neighbor as yourself, you will wish for him the same as you have, the same luxury and comfort that is given to you. If you wish to be perfect, go, sell what you have and give it to the poor and follow me." But the young man went away sorrowful.

Jesus loved this man and wanted to win him. He wanted him as a disciple, and perhaps he might have become a personality of outstanding significance like John, James, or Paul. But he could not be detached from material things, from servitude to mammon. To this young man, mammon meant more than God. The spirit from the abyss, the spirit of dependence on material things, was worth more to him than the Spirit from the heights, the spirit of dependence on God.

This story is of exceptional importance for our time. Of course, it does not mean that everybody should be obliged by law to sell his investments, dispose of his goods, give up his business, and then divide the money among the poor of the city. Jesus tried to show by a thoroughly clear example that conversion to Jesus and to God means a radical separation from mammon, from money.

The point is not whether we give up our property, but that we do no less in any area of life than what is demanded here: that we surrender our money and our life so completely to God that we will be ready – today or tomorrow – to sell our fields and our goods, to give up our business, our investments, and our bank account, and give everything to the Lord and to the poor. The important thing is that we radically reject money and its influence, so that it can no longer dictate to us. We must devote ourselves fully to God with all our income, money, and talents. The spirit of mammon must no longer regulate our relationships with other people, but we must let our lives be ruled by the spirit of love.

EXAMPLES SUCH AS Francis of Assisi are given to us again and again. This man was from a wealthy family and came under the influence of Jesus. He realized that he was vacillating between love for God and love for money, love for his neighbor and love for himself. Then one day he went into the woods. There in a lonely chapel he heard the story of the rich young man, and he was converted to God. He returned to his home town, sold his possessions, his splendid clothing, his horses and carriages. He dressed like the simplest folk and walked from village to village to preach about Jesus and do deeds of love.

There are similar God-given examples in modern times, such as the story of the Russian, Vassili Ossipovich Rachoff (1863–ca. 1905). He too was from a wealthy family, but from childhood on God would not let him go. He was deeply struck by the teachings of Jesus, and one day the story of the rich young man transformed him also. He sold everything he had and walked from village to village. Wherever he went, he lived in the love of God. He did not give long sermons, but simply served in the spirit of Jesus. Where a poor woman was ill, he helped her; where a yard was dirty, he cleaned it up. Soon, in every district he passed through, he became the most beloved and revered person. But the cross came to him too. He was urged by the Spirit to protest against the pious lies of his people, until eventually he was thrown into prison where he was tortured until he collapsed. The witness of this man still has its effect today. Just as he met his death with a childlike simplicity – the world would say childish joy – so his witness was a call to go as a disciple of Jesus, serving with love and turning hearts from mammon to God.

To tell a different example, I know of a wealthy man who owned factories and had millions at his disposal, but who was so unpretentious that he wore the same suits for years until they attracted attention because they were threadbare. He kept his enterprises and did not give all his property away at once, but he did not use this wealth for himself. He administered every penny of it conscientiously and unpretentiously for Christ and his gospel. God gives us such examples so that we can see what it means to decide between mammon and God.

It would be a great mistake to think that only those who control large sums of money are endangered. Jesus shows us that there are different forms of mammonism. They do not depend on our will; the movement of heart is the same in both cases. They simply depend on the circumstances of our lives. One person reveals a mammonistic spirit by accumulating wealth and treasures, while another expresses the same dependence on outward things and servitude to them by worry and care. As long as care rules our house, the spirit of Jesus Christ cannot prevail. As long as worry spreads its dark shadow like a spell over us, the sun of Christ and the love of the Father have not dawned in our lives. As long as our hearts are imprisoned by anxiety and distress, we are on mammon's side and not on God's.

Worry brings about sin. A young girl told me that she had had a good job in Berlin but was lured to Hamburg by a seducer, who told her to give up her job and come – she would be even better off there. Once in Hamburg, he demanded a large sum of money from her. But because she had no work in Hamburg, she had no salary, and so he abandoned her. She was left in the streets, gripped now by panic and fear, and this drove her to sell and defile her body night after night.

Anxiety produces class hatred in us and causes us to clench our teeth and shake our fists when we see others driving by in their expensive cars. It is worry that makes secret triumph arise in our hearts when the blood of the rich is shed, and calls forth hatred, envy, and murderous feelings in us. Worry tempts us to lie in all we do, whether we are poor or rich, avaricious or bound by our fears for survival.

If we are not at home in God's fatherly arms, then we are still the "purchased slaves" of the prince of this world, the father of lies, the murderer from the beginning and his impure spirit. There is only one deliverance: seek first God's kingdom and his righteousness, and all these things shall be yours as well. Jesus says, "Believe in God and believe in me." Believe that God is greater than all money, all outward circumstances. Believe that God cares for you as he does for the flowers in the field and the birds in the trees. Believe that God can clothe you with great splendor, for he loves people as the crown of his creation. Believe that he wants to redeem you from outer trouble and inner worry and fear.

We understand your situation, and know the kind of lying in which you have found yourselves or may find yourselves. I was cut off from my parents' house for some time, and I experienced God's help in a time of severe need. My wife and I have occasionally told with amusement how a maid overheard me praying to God, "God, send us…" and I named a certain sum of money. This girl wrote home that the Arnolds were on the point of bankruptcy: Dr. Arnold was praying for money, and probably there would be something about it in the newspaper. However, nothing appeared in the newspaper. Instead, God sent the money. We often experienced that we received from God what we needed for ourselves and our work without having to ask people. We learned that God cares for us as he does for the birds and the flowers. Every one of us can have this experience and learn this secret. It only depends on our daring to make the plunge into the freedom of the living God and his kingdom. His kingly rulership in our hearts is the freedom we need.

Mammon is not overcome by lying and murder. We are glad that revolutionary movements protest against the mammonistic spirit. We are glad for every protest against devilish mammonism. But at the same time we realize with sorrow that the mammon spirit is also active in these movements, through lying and all kinds of impurity.

There is only one way of finding deliverance from the spirit of mammon and all its evil attributes, and that is through Jesus Christ. Christ on his cross overcame the abyss. He drove out demons through God's spirit and through this proved that God's kingdom had come to us.

Whoever accepts Jesus and his spirit will find that all evil spirits leave him. It depends simply on the question, is there a spirit stronger than the spirit of lying? Is there a spirit stronger than the spirit of impurity, of hate, and of mammon? This is the question that decides your destiny for time and eternity, your hell for today and your hell for eternity.

We are here to witness quite simply to a reality. Yes, there is a Spirit that is stronger than the spirit of lying, impurity, hate, and mammon. That is the spirit of Jesus Christ and his God. Those who receive Christ with heart and soul conquer all the forces of darkness. They have the victory over devilish powers.

Jesus will come one day in his authority and establish his kingdom of peace, joy, and justice on this earth, driving out all evil spirits. This is our hope. Our experience is that already today we have God's kingdom in Jesus Christ. The Lord is the Spirit, and where the spirit of the Lord is, there is freedom.

■ See note for "The Fight Against Mammon," chapter 11.

Resistance by Surrender

THE PERFECT PEACE that appeared in Jesus Christ and his church must, in accordance with the prophets' words, be attacked by all the powers of world economy and by all national governments with their sharpest and deadliest forces. Those who possess the character of unconditional peace go defenseless to their opponent's sword. The kingdom of peace demands readiness to suffer death. Jesus withstands this violence of the whole world with the passive resistance of the cross. The cross against the sword portrays the radicalism of love.

The peace of the Sermon on the Mount attacks the root of sin. Love and sacrifice give the last possessions down to shirt, coat, and cloak, and will quietly double the distance or the working time demanded. The will to peace gives all its working strength, undivided, to total solidarity.

Without letup, the church must actively work against the injustice of public unpeace. In this break with the status quo, Jesus recognizes no justified claims or rights. He does not allow his church to take legal action or to take part in trials. Whenever the honesty of brotherly unity is in question, he commands his followers rather to leave religious exercises than live in a farce of disunited piety.

Jesus commands us never to resist the power of evil, for

this is the only way the evil person can be made good. Jesus' love would rather be struck twice than return a single blow.

In Jesus, love became boundless; it became sovereign, for love surpasses all things. In marriage it remains constant and faithful, combating any separation or divorce. Love permeates hidden prayer as forgiveness. Love determines public conduct and embraces even the enemy – him in particular – for love can never take the slightest part in hostility, quarreling, or war.

Love is not influenced by any hostile power, nor can any outward circumstances sway the attitude of Jesus or his followers. No matter what happens, they show love, practice peace, and do only good. Where the peace of Christ dwells, war, weapons, and hostility disappear.

Here at last the justice of which the prophets spoke takes shape. The justice of Jesus Christ is better than that of all moralists and theologians, better than that of all socialists, communists, and pacifists. For in it flows the sap of a living plant: the peace of the future, the strength of salt. God's living spirit is at work here. The light from God's heart shines out as a beacon from the city on the hill, whose towers proclaim freedom, unity, and surrender. Here all do for others what they wish done for themselves. Here no one gathers a fortune, and no heart grows cold in fear and worry about economic survival; here the peace of love rules.

In this new order the citizens concentrate on one goal: God's will and God's rule, God's heart and his being. No one holds anything against another. No one is condemned and nothing is forced on anyone. No one is despised and no one is violated, because love reigns as truth. The nature of the heart is recognized by its deeds.

It is clear that such a resolute common determination will provoke the keenest antagonism on all sides. The bond of unity that joins and gathers is seen as a provocation. Perceived as hostility and exclusiveness, it excites the indignation of those who, like the masses, are neither able nor willing to accept the call of such complete fellowship. Conflict is unavoidable; no one can escape it.

This living fellowship of hearts, this firm bond between working forces and material goods, contrasts sharply to the conduct of the world. It is bound to cause bitterness in places where people are being recruited for deeds of violence that are ideologically justified. For in this fellowship every hostile action is rejected outright, no matter how justified it seems. All participation in violent police confrontation or judicial proceedings is excluded, however justified on the grounds of protecting the good. Nor can one have anything to do with violent uprisings, even though they seem necessary in the name of justice for the oppressed. The very existence and nature of this life is a challenge to all, right or left, who think that government by force is the highest duty of the hour.

God is unchangeable. His name is "I am who I am." His heart, which was revealed in Jesus Christ – in his words and deeds – enfolds all of creation and remains the same today and forever. What Christ is here and now is the same as what he shall be in his kingdom. The words of his love point to the same way for all things. What Christ said for the future members of his kingdom holds true for his followers of all times. His commands are one and belong together, as the sap and the tree, or the flame and its light.

Therefore Jesus' words about marriage cannot be taken out of the context of the Sermon on the Mount. Jesus represented the will of love in marriage as the will to unity. But this love is revealed just as clearly in freedom from possessions and from judging, in nonviolence and forgiveness, and in love for one's enemies.

Love that is complete presses on to voluntary poverty, because it cannot keep for itself anything that a neighbor lacks. Love is defenseless because it has given up self-preservation and revenge. It remains undaunted and bears evil and wrong for conscience' sake. Nonviolence reveals the love that overcomes all.

Love forgoes everything of its own. Anyone who by a clear conscience protects the mystery of his faith will stay away from any dealings with legal or hostile actions, just as the elders of the early church did. The justice of Christ does not sue, nor will it act as intermediary. It does no business to the disadvantage of its neighbor. It abandons all advantage, sacrifices every privilege, and never defends a right. This justice will not sit on any jury, take away anyone's freedom, or pass a death sentence. It knows no enemies and will not go to war or fight anyone.

Yet this love is constructive and generates the most active justice and peace. The sum total of what we are commanded to do is to love – love with a pure heart, a clear conscience, and a sure faith. Where there is perfect love, Jesus gives free course to the conscience living in fellowship with God.

Jesus' way is the way of agape love. His love tolerates no unclarity, but is distinctly marked and gives a definite direction. Through the experience of God's love, Jesus leads to the highest peak of will power, clear understanding, and the heart's strength, which is joy. He does not do this for our sake. He wants us to pass on to others the streams of love that are poured into our hearts: these streams must flood the earth and conquer the land, disclosing God's heart and establishing his honor.

God's heart and love is his honor. It turns toward all men in the joy of giving. His justice is love. To strive solely for God's kingdom and his justice brings about in us such a love for all people that we want for them the same in all things as we want for ourselves. This alone is justice: to give up our lives for love.

NOTHING BUT THE WHOLE Christ, for the whole of life, will change and renew everything. Half of Jesus for half a life is a delusion, a lie. The spirit of life will not tolerate that a self-willed spirit picks out some principles of faith from God's truth. Truth is indivisible and cannot be dissected. Those who do not take a consistent stand in trying to follow all Christ's commands, reject him. No matter how clever it may be, no justification for their halfhearted behavior will shield them from judgment. "Whoever is not with me is against me."

Some people want to learn just this or that about Christ, and at the same time obliterate or explain away those commands that seem impossible to them. However Christian it may appear, their life will collapse. Jesus says that all who hear his words in the Sermon on the Mount but do not do them, are like those who build on a shifting foundation. What they build is lost from the outset, for it will collapse under the first attack of hostile forces.

Christ, who is whole, wants us whole. He loves decisiveness. He loves his enemies more than his halfhearted friends. He hates those who twist his words more than he hates his opponents. What he abhors is the lukewarm, the colorless gray, the twilight; the foggy, pious talking that mixes everything up and makes no commitments. When he draws near all this is swept away.

He comes to us as he is and penetrates us with his word.

He reveals himself to our hearts in his wholeness. In his coming we feel the power of his love and the strength of his life. Everything else is deception and lying. Jesus Christ never comes close to anyone in a few hasty, fleeting impressions. Either he brings the whole of God's kingdom or he brings nothing. Only those who are willing to receive him completely and forever can experience him. To them it is given to know the secret of God's kingdom. To all others he veils himself in mysterious metaphors. Those who stop short of a full surrender hear parables without understanding what they mean. With seeing eyes, they see nothing; with hearing ears, they understand nothing. Those who do not want to have everything will lose the little they think they have.

True life is the all-inclusive awareness that is able to see deeply into the reality of things and at the same time see out into the distance. True life bears the world's suffering and hungers after justice. For it has heart – God's heart.

God's heart appeared in Jesus, and to God's heart Jesus consecrates the future. All who believe in the future of God's heart are committed from now on to the total will for peace, at any time, in any place.

THE DAWN OF THE NEW TIME lights up the invisible city of peace so that we can see the hidden land of fellowship. In the Holy Spirit of the church, the new Jerusalem comes down. It is the city of perfection, the city without a temple, for its life in fellowship *is* the great King's temple of peace.

The church bears the sevenfold light of the Sabbath of peace, when man's own work shall rest forever because God's great work has quietly begun. The city of peace and joy opens up the brilliance of the new creation. The first things have passed; the last enter with power. Everything becomes new.

The present world can see an image of the city of peace in the church community. This image is a signpost to the future, which all must see. The city of light sends light-bearers out into the world so that no place is left in the dark. The life of the city on the hill is the same as the life of traveling and mission. This light, held high, reaches every corner.

NEW BIRTH is the narrow gate to the kingdom of peace. The liberation of inner peace frees us from dark sin and its curse. This birth sets our eyes on the light of the new world so that we can see God's kingdom. The more starkly we see the contrast between our own weakness and help-lessness on the one hand, and the power and glory of God on the other, the more forcefully will the new life emerge. God's cause takes the place of humanity and its suffering.

The peace of the coming kingdom brings forgiveness; it brings harmony with God's power of love. All the forces of a hitherto divided will are now directed in a new clarity to God and his kingdom. Just as one appreciates the blessing of peace after wartime, so peace of heart depends on the powerful contrast to previous sin and disharmony. Life is possible only through this tension between our own fragmented powerlessness and the energy of God's peace.

THE CENTER FOR the new people is the new hearth of the new church; around it their communal dwelling places arise. Around the radiating fire of the Holy Spirit, their spiritual temple is built up as a tangible house of God. This is the city on the hill whose light beams out into all lands. This place of worship burns in spirit; it shines in truth.

The fire of the Holy Spirit brings the church of glorified martyrs down to the throng of believers gathered around Christ's flaming throne. There is living unity in the flame of the spirit between those who have passed on and those who remain on earth. The unanimity of the people gathered for full community in the house of God is the unity of the church above. It lives in that perfect light to which no mortal life on our shadowy earth has access.

In its glowing love, the spirit of unity takes its leading from the city above. It does not only lead the believers, weak people as they are, to community of goods in possessions, land, and work: it guides them to pass on the flame through hospitality and fire-bearing mission, serving as messengers to all on the earth. Then unity of the church becomes a message of peace for all the world from the kingdom of light.

The Spirit is the mystery of the city on the hill. Apart from the one way – the way of the Spirit that gives unity with the city above – there is no church community on earth. The church community of God lives only in the pure air of its eternal mountain peak. Its citizens and their politics are of heaven. From there this city expects everything, and from there it is ruled.

■ Extracts from the book *Inner Land* by Eberhard Arnold (Rifton, NY: Plough, 1976).

The Spirit of Life Overcomes

THERE ARE SOME who, in spite of earnest efforts toward religion and orthodoxy, are not yet overwhelmed by the unique spirit of Jesus Christ. These do not belong to the church community of Christ, nor to the mission. This is a painful fact for many. For the only way they know to help themselves is to try honestly to love other people and see to their own salvation. But these people do not belong to God's kingdom. This is terribly frightening, but it is true.

Only the chosen, the sought-out, belong to God's kingdom and Christ's church community – those who by God's grace have been given the spirit that is wholly different. This is the spirit that does not strive for personal holiness, personal salvation; that does not try to become good or seem good. It is the spirit that recognizes and honors God and his demands.

With the exception of the Sermon on the Mount, in which he told clearly what counts, Jesus expressed this mystery in parables. The Sermon on the Mount can be compared to a tree that God himself has planted, a sap that our blood cannot produce, a salt that we cannot manufacture – its nature is given by God. It represents a light that we cannot kindle, an essence that comes to us alone from the fount of God's being.

The Sermon on the Mount has been a mystery impossible for many of its advocates to understand. There is no new set of laws here, no new commandments or prohibitions replacing the old Ten Commandments. Here the new tree, the new light, the new salt, the new essence reveal God's heart as it was given to humankind in Jesus Christ, and as it will rule in his coming kingdom.

The Lord's prayer to God is the central focus of this new light. It calls for his kingdom to come, for his rule to break in, for his being to be revealed and honored, for his will to be done. The whole gospel is integrated into this call – the request for daily bread, both spiritual and temporal; the assurance of forgiveness of sin; the freeing of the whole earth from the might of the devil; and protection in the hour of temptation that will come over the earth.

Therefore, the demand for human action and decision is central to the Sermon on the Mount. Your innermost vision must be changed to see differently. Until now you have only been seeing cross-eyed; your inward eye has been looking in all different directions at once. Different desires and concerns have animated you at each moment, and you have not been able to concentrate on the one single thing and be true to it. But now your inner eye must become single. You must become completely simple, com-

pletely decided for the one cause, that is, for God's kingdom and his justice.

For this you must have no property. You must not
gather wealth that would divert your eye from God's rule
and God's justice. But you must have no worries either.
The spirit of worry about your livelihood, about the small
details of food, clothing, and shelter, must never enslave
you. Freedom from possessions is what this spirit demands – this pure spirit that wants nothing but God's
rulership and justice. You ought to be so free from these
material things that you feel like flowers and birds that
have been clothed and fed since the beginning of creation
without planting or sowing, plowing or tilling.

Only those who immerse themselves completely in God
and his command can find this freedom from possessions
and the spirit of care. For them the words "Do not judge!"
are a decision against all legal institutions, and they do not
go to law. They would rather take off coat and cloak than
quarrel about such outward things. They would rather
work overtime than refuse a request for help or a request
to walk an extra mile. They go out of their way to meet
their enemies so as not to allow any spark of hostile, judg-
mental fire into their own hearts. They know that singleness of heart and purpose allows no exaggerated words,
no swearing of oaths, including those sworn before authorities or courts. They speak simply and truthfully

without idle phrases or rhetoric, saying neither more nor less than what is necessary.

God's spirit gives the clarity that makes hostility and enmity impossible. Here is winning love, perfect love, the love that through the inward glow of the heart draws all – including opponents – into the sphere of love. Evil is combated here not by resisting it forcibly, but by not allowing its principles to find their way into life's struggle.

Evil is combated only by means of good, through love. So also in the realm of human love, complete clarity must rule. No unfaithfulness in human relationships can arise, no greed for variety prompted by lustful desire can take root. Instead, single-heartedness must be the rule, the unity of two in Christ-centered marriage. Then any covetousness that makes the eye look sideways is recognized as out-and-out sin and done away with.

This is the secret of an attitude that knows only one law – perfect, pure love – evident in all areas of life. This is the Sermon on the Mount.

For this reason, Jesus makes a sharp distinction between the different spirits, in opposition to the weakness that says yes to everything (or no to everything). He demands a clear "yes" to what is important – God's kingdom and his justice – and therefore a clear "no" to all other influences. Test the spirits! By their works and their fruits you will recognize them. It is not what a person says that determines the spirit in him, but what he or she does – the outcome of his practical work – that reveals the cause he serves.

TWO ANIMALS IN CREATION show us the decisive contrast: the wolf portrays the sneaking nature of the beast of prey; the sacrificial lamb, the spirit of solidarity and sacrifice. The lamb's nature knows what serves the whole flock. All works must be tested as to whether they demonstrate the nature of the beast of prey that lusts and lacerates and wants to possess and kill, or the nature of the lamb that stands ready for sacrifice.

In the Sermon on the Mount Jesus sums up the call to go through the narrow gate. Treat others as you wish them to treat you. Struggle to get for all whatever you need for yourself: the physical necessities of life or the needs of soul and spirit. That is the small gateway, the narrow path. Whatever you do, think of the whole. Whatever you achieve, achieve it for everyone. We must act according to these words, for if we do not, the structure of our life will topple in ruins. But anyone who does obey will build on rock, for he lives from the spirit of Jesus Christ. This is the way of Jesus that we are called to go.

We should not become anxious or cowardly. Let us not give up but be courageous, taking reality as it is. It is simply a fact that any group of people on this earth will have many imperfections, shortcomings, and weaknesses, and lack gifts in all possible areas. Anyone who knows anything at all about human life must realize that it simply cannot be otherwise.

The first thing, then, is that we cannot make superhuman demands of one another. That would be unfair. It would lead us into a legalism and moralism that despises others who do not have the same gifts. This evil spirit of arrogance is the greatest enemy; we must thoroughly banish it from our midst. We must have the humility and courage to be small, knowing that even if a person has more gifts in one area, the same person may have fewer gifts in another. We need to be able to bear with one another in love and daily forgiveness; otherwise community is impossible. For there will never be a group of human beings with gifts so perfectly attuned that no conflicts can arise due to human weakness. Nowhere is there such a thing on this earth.

That is the first thing. But the second is equally important. Our sober insight must never make us lose faith, for that would mean losing everything. It is our faith that the Holy Spirit, who penetrates our inmost being, also wants to bring all outward circumstances under his rule. We believe that the boundary line between the one and the other does not lie between spirit and matter, or depth of faith and material work. It is our belief that this boundary passes right through the spiritual as well as the material, through economy and finance as well as through Christian piety.

This is our faith: the spirit of innermost peace and unity can master all outward aspects of work and living. The only limitation (mentioned before) is the lack of human gifts. Only to the extent that human stubbornness and weakness come to the fore will the picture be imperfect. But as far as God and the Spirit are concerned, this penetration is complete. To the extent that we believe the Holy Spirit and allow it to pervade every aspect of our lives, the building up of the cause to serve as many people as possible will be complete. To the extent that the Holy Spirit rules in the outward aspects of our work and life, the church of Jesus Christ will give a true picture of God's kingdom.

It is just as Paul says in Romans, chapter 7: "Who will set me free from this body of death? I am not able to do what I would so much like to do. Again and again I do the evil I do not want to do at all. In myself as a human being I can find no good." But after the seventh chapter comes the eighth, and here we read that there can be no condemnation for those who are in Christ Jesus. No judgment can be carried out on them, for what is born of God overcomes the world. "The law of life in the spirit of Christ Jesus has set me free from the natural law of sin and death."

According to this eighth chapter, the spirit of life overcomes and rules material nature, which is subject to the natural law of death. We must believe in this! But it can take place only through the spirit of humility and love, for that is the spirit of Jesus Christ. It can take place only if, together with groaning creation, we set our eyes on the end so that we see the dazzling splendor of the throne of God's kingdom and the deliverance of the sons of God. This is why the church exists: to dare to start *now* with this future, perfect world of God's kingdom.

The same apostle says, "God's kingdom already now consists in justice, peace, and joy; it exists through the Holy Spirit." The will to perfect love depends on faith in the Holy Spirit, faith that despite our human weakness the Spirit can fill our hearts with glowing love, conquering and penetrating our work, our relationships, and our creative powers.

IN SHORT, the first secret of the Sermon on the Mount – the singleness of the inner eye – must show itself in practical life. So we want the greatest simplicity possible in everything we do. Our goal is simple clarity of conduct liberated from the gathering of treasures. The more plainly and simply we give shape to our work, the more we will reveal the true picture of God's kingdom and its deepest meaning.

If we allow things to tyrannize us, we will be lost. We must put them in the hands of the Holy Spirit; then everything will fit together. By simplifying our life, we will be able to serve more people and take better care of all material goods so that they are available for those still to come.

Jesus prayed, not only for those who were entrusted to him, but also for those still to be won in the future by the word of the apostles. Our daily work must be protected so that everything we do is a loving prayer for all those who may come to the church, even years later, through the witness of our work and be provided by the church with shelter, clothing, and food. This must be our watchword of love: whatever you expect from the community for yourself, do the same for all others, including those who are still to come in the future!

If we are newly gathered in the complete unanimity of this simple, loving spirit, all conflict among us will be resolved. Then we will be able to give one another the greeting of "peace and unity" with courage and joy. We will not need to fear political persecutions. If the joy of our deepest unity fills our hearts, we will not be afraid of anyone.

The reverence of perfect love drives out the fear of men.
Whoever fears God fears no man. And perfect love drives
out fear.

■ From a talk, October 22, 1933, when the Rhön Bruderhof faced increasing hostility from the Nazi regime.

Present Experience, Future Kingdom

JOHN THE BAPTIST proclaimed the future state of social justice, God's kingdom, which shall come to this earth. Like all prophets, he wanted to pave the way for the conditions to come by transforming hearts and deeds. His call to repentance demanded a complete revolution of the inner and outer life. He wanted to remove the obstacles of personal and social wrong that keep the individual from God's kingdom. He insisted on complete transformation because he believed that God's kingdom was near. What mattered to him were the real fruits of repentance: simple, plain morality. When the people asked John what they should do, he said that absolute surrender was the only way to social justice: "If someone has two coats, let him share with him who has none; and if he has food, let him do likewise."

Though crowds of people came to be baptized by him and find forgiveness and renewal, John knew that another had to bring the transforming, sanctifying Spirit, without which the new conditions could not take root. This other was the longed-for Messiah, the just, peacemaking king of God's kingdom. The greatest event in the Baptist's life therefore was the realization that this anticipated Messiah had appeared in Jesus. The work of Jesus grew out of the activity of John the Baptist's prophetic proclamation. Jesus took up John's message literally, and he too was directed by the imminence of God's kingdom. Everything he had to say was closely related to an earthly revolution, which he expected from God.

Jesus indeed baptized in the spirit. If we allow his words to work on us we are gripped by a refreshing wind that penetrates our body. He adds a new sphere of life, a strength and joy never known to us before. About God's kingdom Jesus said, "What is born of the flesh is flesh, and what is born of the Spirit is spirit." "Anyone who is not born of water and the Spirit cannot enter the kingdom of God." Jesus declared that without this new birth a vision for the future kingdom is impossible. In this, as in everything else, he lived in the prophetic truth that society can be transformed only through a moral renewal of the spiritual life.

Jesus told us more clearly than any of the prophets what the characteristics of this spirit are, without which we can gain neither inner renewal nor the future state on earth. In the Sermon on the Mount, Jesus defines the implications of his proclamation, "Repent, for the kingdom is at hand."

We all know the Beatitudes, where the poor, the suffering, the merciful, and the loving are blessed and shall inherit the kingdom of heaven. Yet how few consider what form this earthly kingdom should take in accordance with the will of the preacher on the mount. How few see the moral demands implied when only those are called blessed who give their lives for peace and justice. Are there more than a handful of people who realize the ethical implications of this?

We realize that no moral law can demand an absolute will for peace or an absolute justice of love. Nobody will have the courage to make such demands on himself or on others. Yet no one was less moralistic than Jesus. The new justice – better than moralism and coercion – shall penetrate the world like salt and light, working freely and spontaneously. The light would be dark and the salt insipid if love no longer controlled our lives. God's kingdom is the kingdom of love. Its principles make no exceptions or qualifications, because love is free life-energy and cannot be held back.

Anyone gripped by the spirit of God's kingdom is so liberated from any murderous impulses that it would be impossible for him to injure human dignity or live unreconciled with another. This perfect love and respect means faithfulness, above all in engagement and marriage. Its only weapons are joyful dedication and genuine relationships with all others. That is why this love turns the other cheek and gives away the coat as well as the jacket. It shows love to neighbor and enemy alike, helps without restraint, and gives its blessing unconditionally.

Into this love Jesus immerses his friends, so that they no longer live in any other atmosphere. This spirit of love blows like a fresh wind of truthfulness, honesty, and simplicity. It has nothing to do with unhealthy emotionalism or introspection. That is why Jesus hates sensational activity and wants to be unobtrusive in all he does. In communing with God and with people, he is simple and concise.

The sharp divisions in the life of an individual and between people now become clear. Jesus' divine spirit of love stands in opposition to the spirit of mammon and its will to power. He commands us: do not lay up treasures on earth for yourself. Only the heart firmly decided for God, the self-disciplined soul seeking the highest goal, can be liberated from self-seeking and bondage of any kind. If the justice of the future divine state is our only longing, then we are truly free from worry and from our degenerate, self-centered life. To experience this justice means being flooded by love, and brings a sensitivity to the inner and outer necessities of our fellowmen, so that we want the same good for them as we would want for ourselves.

Though generally known to Christians, the Sermon on the Mount has remained completely unrecognized by them. Yet in the Sermon on the Mount Jesus characterizes the inner life which alone can bring about a true social life among men – the life of God's future state. The Sermon on the Mount is the secret of God's kingdom, and as such can only be revealed in God himself. We can hope for and take hold of the future kingdom only in communion with God. The prayer in this "sermon" is therefore the Lord's Prayer.

IT IS INCREDIBLE DISHONESTY in the human heart to pray daily that this kingdom should come, that God's will be done on earth as in heaven, and at the same time to deny that Jesus wants this kingdom to be put into practice on earth. Whoever asks for the rulership of God to come down on earth must believe in it and be wholeheartedly resolved to carry it out. Those who emphasize that the Sermon on the Mount is impractical and weaken its moral obligations should remember the concluding words, "Not all who say 'Lord' to me shall reach the kingdom of heaven, but only those who do the will of my Father in heaven."

Many think that Jesus warped the message of the Sermon on the Mount in his parables in such a way that he no longer spoke of a future state, but only of a present sphere of influence of God's kingdom. But these people misjudge the crucial content of Jesus' message. They try to reconcile the supposed contradictions of the parables so that their interpretation of God's future limits his working in the present, which they consider to be weakened and adapted. Jesus, however, speaks in parables because only these paradoxical pictures are able to convey the absolute as the basic experience of God's kingdom.

The kingdom of God is absolute, its love unconditional, and its social justice perfect. We are surrounded by the relative, the imperfect, the conditional – all that accommodates itself to circumstances. Whoever lives, like Jesus, in the absolute, the unconditional, and the perfect, possesses God and his kingdom in the present. That is why Jesus testified that in his person the kingdom of God had arrived among men. Because his experience of the absolute was unfeigned, his life was free of the influences of his surroundings. What he was in himself, and what he possessed, had a forming and transforming effect on his environment; therefore his healing of the sick is an essential part of the picture of Jesus. That is also why, when he sent out his messengers with the barest necessities, healing the sick and raising the dead was a necessary condition to show the genuineness of their message that the kingdom of God was at hand.

Believing in the absolute will of God for the present is the same as expecting his kingdom. The same intensity of inner experience belongs to both. Both depend so much on each other that through a present attitude of absolute love, the future expectation of perfect justice is given, and vice versa. However, as in all genuine experiences of the eternal, this can never be a matter of defining the future in terms of periods of time. The Spirit reaches across all spaces – eliminating all distance and time – at one with the God-given future.

Like scattered seed, this experience spontaneously creates the corresponding attitude of perfect love. This can be choked by care, wealth, and mammon – the enemies of spontaneous life – only if the will is open to their hostile influence. Like an organic growth, the kingdom of God begins as a single seed. Yet the more it unfolds, the more joy and help it can give. It is difficult to know where the Spirit is quietly unfolding since it is a delicate spiritual process, particularly in its initial stages. Thus weeds and wheat must grow together until the harvest.

The new life is like a precious pearl, a buried treasure of immense value to be won only by those who give up everything for it. A follower of Christ gives his life in unreserved love and devotion, in work for peace and social justice. Such a life influences the great world as leaven works in dough. Yet leaven can only do this if it stays unadulterated, if it keeps its full strength.

Only this perfect spirit of the Sermon on the Mount makes it possible to experience the kingdom of God. In the parable of the talents, the unity between present experience and the future state is clearly shown: whoever has worked in this world, vigorously using the divine powers entrusted to him, shall be put in charge of broad lands and cities in the future state.

THE KINGDOM OF GOD cannot be of the world as it is to-day. Yet it is *for* the world, in order to exercise the strongest effect on it and in the end transform it completely. Christ's people are sent out to work among humanity, to have an effect in the world, just as Jesus himself did. They must represent the message of the future kingdom, and their task and their actions cannot be different from Christ's: to bring help and deliverance for soul and body, to heal and help in all sufferings and torments.

Like Jesus, his people must overcome the temptation to produce bread by evil means or win control in the realm of politics. All this is contrary to God's spirit. They have been sent like defenseless sheep among ravenous wolves, and they reject all ways of aggression. In obedience to the word of their Lord they have sheathed their swords; love and the Spirit are their only weapons. They know that this spirit of Jesus is the mightiest power, which no other power can withstand. He who sent them does not want to destroy life but to save it, and, as children of the spirit, they cannot forget to which spirit they belong. So, too, they cannot send destructive fire on people and cities. The only fire Jesus kindled is the fire of love. There was nothing he wanted more than that this warming light and fire spread over the whole earth.

Jesus knew the resistance in the spiritual realm that had to be overcome before victory could be won. The life of

God can be won only by complete firmness of will – the absolute can be won only by totality. This is why the old, degenerate life must be abhorred to gain the new life. One must hate father and mother, wife and child – indeed, one's own life wherever it disturbs and destroys the new life.

This is why Jesus advised the rich young man to sell his possessions, follow him, and live for the poor, and why he himself did not have anywhere to sleep. Jesus said to his friends, "Sell what you have and do justice…Whoever does not renounce all he has cannot be my disciple."

To see this as negating earthly things is to misjudge what is real and essential. Jesus contrasts the richness of gathering treasures with the richness of life in God. Bringing in the richest harvest or erecting the biggest buildings cannot benefit us if we lose eternal life. Ownership or abundance of earthly goods can never give life. To find true happiness on earth we must beware of the love of money in every form. Our richness consists in this: each day we are allowed to live, filled with God's love and gathering treasure in heaven, is a gift from God.

Money, which Jesus calls unjust mammon, has only one advantage: to make friends through love that shares and gives away. For love, which makes life fully alive, must generate love. It is life's only wealth. The man who has overcome his selfishness gains his life. Jesus says that to love God is the greatest love in a person's life and exists wherever we love our fellowmen as much as we love ourselves. Those who do not have this love, however much piety they may show, lack the most important thing: the sense for justice, mercy, and faithfulness.

Whoever lives in this spirit draws the kingdom of God into the present. Where this spirit is alive, the kingdom of God rushes in violently and is won by storm. It reveals itself everywhere as good news for the poor, liberation for the oppressed, enslaved, and imprisoned. It reveals such a victory over discrimination and hatred that the poor and incapacitated are invited rather than the rich and the relatives; and the strongest love and justice goes to social outcasts. Jesus had the greatest compassion for the sick and the sinners. Those who have his spirit feel drawn to the victims of discrimination and prejudice, and to those who suffer either through their own guilt or that of others. Whoever experiences this justice of love will never feel like a benefactor condescendingly distributing alms, but will know the fulfillment of his deepest calling in service and interdependence with all people.

Jesus says that such people are not even conscious of the Christlike character of their lives. They live for the hungry and the thirsty, the homeless and the naked, the sick and the imprisoned. Yet they do not know what they have done until they are told, "Whatever you have done to one of these, the least of my brothers, you have done to me." This life is so deeply immersed in the spirit of brotherliness that nobody strives for a high position. They seek only for the simplest way of serving and helping as many as they can. Whoever lies by the roadside and is in need is my neighbor, and to him I give my love.

My enemies are those who either suffer because of me, or who inflict great harm on themselves because of their hostility. Such people need to be loved especially. Their resistance can only be overcome by a stream of genuine affection, by acts of practical service, and by honest intercession. That is why antagonism should be overcome at the outset by offering the enemy every possible settlement before it can come to a lawsuit or a state of war.

A life of this nature is possible only if we can repeatedly become young again – spontaneous and trusting. Only a life born out of unconstrained feeling, out of childlike, genuine emotion, loving all people the way children do, is capable of such an attitude. Only through this same childlike trust can we become one with God. Jesus said, "Whoever does not receive the kingdom of God like a child cannot enter." The kingdom of God belongs to the young and to the childlike.

YOUTH IS STORMY. Young people love what is absolute and true, genuine and spontaneous. This is why young people are the revolutionaries of whom Jesus says they seize the kingdom as if by violence. Since Jesus came, the kingdom of God rushes in with force wherever it is taken by storm.

It is the same as with a man buried alive in an earthquake. In the foul, lethally compressed air, he suddenly manages to break an opening, and the fresh air rushes in. At that moment the man feels completely united with the world he is longing for, even though he is still unable to step into it. In the same way we, who are imprisoned in the present moment, are overwhelmed by the powers of eternity as soon as we dare to draw to ourselves the eternal and absolute, the divine and perfect.

■ Published as "Das Gegenwartserlebnis des Zukunftreiches" in *Das neue Werk,* 1919.

The Joyful News
of the Kingdom

CHAPTER SEVENTEEN

WHEN WE FEEL too weak to do what is asked of us, then we lack the love of Christ, the love poured into our hearts by the Holy Spirit. This love has none of the unclarity of human thinking and feeling, but is clear in what it wants.

The love of Jesus is made completely clear by his life. The power of Jesus' life, sealed by the Holy Spirit in his death and resurrection, was poured out on the first church in Jerusalem. This is the Spirit of whom it was foretold that he would recall the words of Jesus and throw clear light on his life; he would reveal the future and convict the world of sin in righteousness and judgment. Sin was revealed as unbelief in Jesus. Righteousness was revealed by the Holy Spirit through the fact that Jesus is seated on the throne of God and brings the rulership of the eternal kingdom. Judgment was revealed through the prince of this world being judged by the love of Jesus Christ. This prince is the spirit of the times, who controls all peoples. He is the spirit of might who is named a liar and murderer from the beginning. He was judged by the love of Jesus Christ, not by a forcible, violent deed, but because Jesus in his living and dying was revealed as the best, the most loving one.

Whoever takes the side of Jesus is free from the spirit of this world that has been judged. Those who want to follow that spirit yield to deceitfulness, lying, and unfaithfulness, and are judged along with it. Whoever wants to follow Jesus does not accept destruction or any work of the devil.

Wherever the church of Jesus really exists, the Holy Spirit reigns as the revelation of Jesus Christ. He discloses what the future of Jesus means. All this and more has been revealed through the outpouring of the Spirit. This is made clear in the life of Jesus. What Jesus did, and what he said, revealed perfect love. First of all it is evident that Jesus is the perfect love of God. Everything he did was born out of this love. Because of this love he accepted baptism by John, consecrating himself to death.

His love for God was victorious in the threefold temptation. The prince of this world, the tempter, challenged him to take possession of the world's thrones by allying himself with the spirit of lying and impurity. The tempter challenged him to proclaim his greatness by prevailing over the law of gravity in the presence of all the people. He wanted Christ to make himself popular by feeding the people abundantly with bread.

But Jesus loved God, his father, above all. He drove Satan off and brought God's kingdom into action, not by ruling the earth or by winning humankind over as such, but by the power of his love for God. "Be gone, Satan! You shall serve God alone. Man does not live by bread alone, but by every rousing word from God's loving heart."

This is the word he proclaimed: God is all that matters! He alone must rule; prepare yourselves for this! There are mighty events in human history, but none of them comes anywhere near the coming of God. When God's kingdom comes, that will be historic!

This is the crucial thing: Love him! Change yourselves and your lives and the way you think. Everything must topple. Believe the joyful news and repent: "The kingdom of God is at hand!" God is near!

JESUS PROCLAIMED THIS GOOD NEWS not only through parables. He also stated its meaning in clear, unmistakable words: God is coming; his rulership is approaching. The Gospel of John, speaking of Nicodemus, says that man must be renewed in such a way that he begins all over again like a baby. He must be born again; a completely new beginning must be made. New birth has meaning only in the sense of being born anew for God's kingdom. Without it no one can enter God's kingdom – this alone is what counts.

The nature of the new beginning is described in Matthew's Gospel. The Sermon on the Mount shows that

rebirth into a new life brings a righteousness and a goodness that is incomparably better than any morals, theol-
ogy, or anything that has ever been said or thought. This
new righteousness is God's doing; it is the outpouring of
his spirit, the essence of the light that is to come, the salti-
ness of salt. It is essence and power, life in the fullest sense,
freedom in movement.

Before people can find this new life of righteousness,
they must be poor as beggars. They must take the world's
suffering upon themselves, desire peace in a peaceless
world, and long for goodness and love. They must be
ready for sacrifice, even death. If they are willing to suffer
for his justice and his kingdom, then they will know God's
heart; they will find God himself.

Here the knowledge of God's kingdom begins: enemies
are loved, the last penny is given away, and violence is
never repaid with force. Purity and faithfulness belong to
love. This is the better righteousness, the complete love.

"You should be perfect like the Father." There is no
other perfection, only that of love. So be aware of the
things that thwart this love: property and worry! Wherever possessions are heaped up while elsewhere people go
hungry and cold, there is no love. So gather no wealth
for yourself. Do not worry. Worriers build life on wealth
just as much as the wealthy. Look at the birds and flowers,
and believe in the loving God, the Father who provides
everything.

What you need is an undivided heart, an eye that focusses on God alone. Then you will have no wealth and no worry. You will understand that to call upon God in prayer means to trust in his love, implore his rulership, do his will, and honor his name. This is your daily bread. Through this prayer you will be freed from evil and temptation. This is how you must call to God.

You must love all people, but that does not mean that you reveal what is holiest in your heart to those who are not ready for it. Neither must you judge them, for that would be sinning against love for God and love for people. God's love is greater than your condemnation. He knows the hearts of the guilty. So treat them as you yourself would wish to be treated. You want God to provide for you; therefore do for everyone without exception what you expect for yourself. You should set no limits to the deeds you do out of love. After all, God loves human beings no matter what they are like. Truth expressed in loving deeds – this is the narrow gate, the entry into God's kingdom. It is the only true reality in your life. When you care for others in body, soul, and spirit as you care for yourself, then you will know the gate to the kingdom of God.

Pursue this way even if there are only very few of you. Disturbing spirits and powers will try to thwart you, but you will know the false prophets by their predatory nature. True prophets can be recognized by their lamb-like nature and their love – the love that gives up life itself for brothers and sisters.

THE HOSTILITY TO JESUS soon became severe. His opponents used such guile and cunning to try to entrap him by theological argument that, after sending out the apostles, he spoke only in parables. These were meant to veil the truth from the meddlesome and impudent who listened only to confute. To hearts that were open he disclosed the entire mystery of the kingdom of God. He revealed its ultimate meaning in the parables of the wedding and the banquet, which were symbols of the fellowship of sharing all that is entrusted to us by God.

God's kingdom consists in action and is therefore compared to the workers in the vineyard. The point is to do "yes" even though one may say "no." The sower is needed to plant the seed so that it can multiply, blessed by heaven. Only through our complete readiness to respond can the kingdom of love, unity, and work be attained.

The new kingdom cannot be patched onto the garment of the old kingdom. Everything must be given away for the priceless jewel, the kingdom of God. The only path to God's kingdom is to sell everything and leave it.

At first the kingdom is like leaven in dough, worked into the entire substance of human life. It is like a grain of seed. But it grows, and growing it becomes like a tree beneath which everything can live. Even though the enemy may scatter his counterfeit seed among the good seed, do not use force. Both must be left to grow until the harvest.

The citizens of this kingdom must be like the kingdom itself: strong like a rock and fruitful like a tree. They must have the love and joy described in the banquet and the wedding feast, and the inward readiness that we see in the parable of the virgins. They must be tenacious, vigilant, and faithful like the loyal steward and servant in the parable. They must be active in love and not indulge in their own pleasure, as in the parable of the rich man.

Humble hearts, free of all self-importance, are their first characteristic, like the man in the temple who cried out, "God have mercy on me, sinner that I am!" The citizen of the kingdom possesses a heart that looks for the strayed sheep, accepts the prodigal son back into the household, and seeks to bring people into fellowship with God before the door is closed. Here is the true flock, the true shepherd, the true pasture. Here is real community. Love for the individual and for the whole – this is love to God. The mystery of the kingdom can be compared to the organic unity of a vine: the individuals are the branches, the vine is Christ himself and his Holy Spirit.

Christ sums up his truth in sharpest opposition to false prophecy. His love radically rejects and combats evil. He cries out the sevenfold "Woe!" and proclaims the catastrophe of God's judgment on all who betray and forsake him.

Because of these words he was executed as an enemy of the people, an enemy of the best state and the best church.

JESUS DID EVERYTHING that he talked about. His whole life demonstrated love, especially in gathering his disciples and sending them out. He showed that he was able to carry the burden of fellowship: he persevered with them in a communal life of complete sharing. The Gospels were written out of this daily discourse of Jesus, in which he explained everything through his parables and teachings. As John writes at the end of his Gospel, Jesus did many more things, but if they were all written down the world could not hold the books that would have to be filled.

While Jesus was among his disciples and friends, he proved his love by what he did for body, soul, and spirit, according to their degree of readiness. He healed people of leprosy and skin diseases; the blind saw, the lame walked, and the man with the withered arm was healed. He took away fever, made the deaf-mute hear and speak, and straightened the deformed woman. Bodies already in corruption were raised from death: Lazarus, the young man at Nain, and the little daughter of Jairus. His actions demonstrated what it will be like when God's kingdom comes. The driving out of demons and the healing of sickness belong to the conquest of the spirit of death.

Along with all this, Jesus proved God's love by mastering the elements. He fed the four thousand and the five thousand, calmed the storm, and transformed water into wine as a sign of his love and of his participation in joy.

The many things Jesus did showed that outward healing is a symbol of something even greater and more crucial – a demonstration that the love of God will do everything that belongs to love, also for people's bodies. Matter is not excluded from God's kingdom and his rule.

At the same time God's love turns toward the inward life so as to prepare the soul for his kingdom. Go, and do evil no more! By healing both outwardly and inwardly, Jesus manifested his authority to forgive. Forgiveness is healing – it is removal of evil. Healing is the symbol of forgiveness; it is the sign that when Jesus comes the power of evil is conquered. This is why resurrection from the dead had to happen. God had to be demonstrated as unconquerable life. Death is the last enemy and must be defeated if God is to rule.

God is life because God is love. God is love because he is life. As such he is resurrection. Jesus therefore rose from the dead and was revealed as the living One. He was present in the outpouring of the Holy Spirit when these words were fulfilled: "I am with you all the days." The king of the kingdom is the Spirit. The king of God's kingdom and the spirit of the church are one. Jesus with his whole authority is present wherever the Holy Spirit of love is at work. This is the certainty of the gospel.

■ Spoken during a worship meeting at the Alm Bruderhof on May 4, 1934.